MIRACLES

Above: *The resurrection of Lazarus. This painting by Giotto depicts the miracle of Jesus raising Lazarus from the dead.*

MIRACLES

The Extraordinary, the Impossible and the Divine

VIKING
STUDIO
BOOKS

MIRACLES

A LABYRINTH BOOK

VIKING STUDIO BOOKS

Published by the Penguin Group
Penguin Books USA Inc., 375 Hudson Street, New York, New York 10014, U.S.A.
Penguin Books Ltd, 27 Wrights Lane, London W8 5TZ, England
Penguin Books Australia Ltd, Ringwood, Victoria, Australia
Penguin Books Canada Ltd, 10 Alcorn Avenue, Toronto, Ontario, Canada M4V 3B2
Penguin Books (N.Z.) Ltd, 182 - 190 Wairau Road, Auckland 10, New Zealand
Penguin Books Ltd, Registered Offices: Harmondsworth, Middlesex, England

First published in 1995 by Viking Penguin, a division of Penguin Books USA Inc.

10 9 8 7 6 5 4 3 2 1

LIBRARY OF CONGRESS CATALOGING-IN-PUBLICATION DATA

Neiman, Carol.
Miracles: the extraordinary, the impossible, and the divine
Carol Neiman.
p.   cm.
ISBN 0-670-85582-0
1. Miracles. I.Title.
BL487.N45 1995

21-dc20   94-23016

Printed in Italy.
Designed and typeset by Gail D'Almaine, in association with Generation Associates

CONTENTS

Part One
Defining the Indefinable

miracle *n.* [L. miraculum *fr.* mirari, to wonder at] **1.** an extraordinary event manifesting divine intervention in human affairs **2.** an extremely outstanding or unusual event, thing or accomplishment **3.** Christian Science: a divinely natural occurrence that must be learned humanly

The Extraordinary...

As Webster's Dictionary shows us, the primary definition of a miracle is related to something extraordinary, something far beyond the normal course of events in ordinary life, something inspiring perhaps and amazing certainly. But the occurrence is not only amazing but also divine in nature. It includes the intervention of a force outside what we regard as day-to-day activity. When it occurs, a miracle astonishes us.

We are not talking here about the kinds of miracles that we might refer to with exclamations in the secular usage familiar to us in such expressions as, "It was a miracle he passed his exams," or "It will take a miracle to get them out of debt." The word

miracle has gained popular use in our ordinary world just as the word divine has come to be used in the vernacular to express non-religious hyperbole. What we need to do to get into the frame of "mind" needed to feel the power of the miracle is to step back a moment and try to assimilate the original sense of the miraculous as it was felt by those that genuinely experienced events that were perpetrated by the presence of real divinity. When Webster's Dictionary refers to "an extremely outstanding or unusual event, thing or accomplishment" this is perhaps intended to denote a sense of "extremely outstanding" at a level beyond the passing of examinations or the paying of debts. One of the problems of twentieth-century

Above: *Joshua commanding the sun to stand still. This Old Testament miracle is dramatically portrayed in this painting by John Martin.*

life may be perceived as resulting from the religious disillusionment of mankind as a whole, perhaps partly due to the overbearing presence of science, and therefore the use of what were inspired words to describe mundane events.

Finally, the Christian Science sect founded by Mary Baker Eddy takes particular credit in Webster's Dictionary for a view of the miraculous that has now grown far beyond the Christian Science Church. It suggests that we can all become miracle-workers once we get over the idea that it is either impossible or undesirable for us to do so.

The first aspect, then, of the miraculous to be taken up in our search for a definition, is this extraordinariness. A miracle is, in the words of St. Thomas Aquinas "apart from the generally established order of things." So much "apart," in fact, that it stops us in our tracks, wakes us up from our sleep, shocks us out of our tendency to function on automatic pilot as we go through the routines of our day. To quote Aquinas again, referring to the Latin root of the word, these events "are customarily called miracles, for we admire with some astonishment a certain event when we observe the effect but do not know the cause."

That is not the whole definition, of course. It might be extraordinary that a poor student passes his exams, and the odds against winning the lottery and thereby being able to pay off one's debts might

be overwhelming, but these things are not really "miracles" unless there is something more to them than unexpected good fortune, something perhaps divine. Furthermore, just because we "observe the effect but do not know the cause" is not necessarily enough to astonish us. Trees grow to incredible heights from tiny seeds, and the cocoon woven by last year's caterpillar opens in the spring to reveal a butterfly—few people understand how these things happen, but as we grow older we grow accustomed to them. They are miraculous in the sense of being wondrous, but they reveal themselves, through constant repetition, to be within the "generally established order of things." The extraordinary, therefore, in this context, is really so extraordinary that we probably cannot actually believe it possible.

The impossibility of miracles has been a particularly troublesome feature of their history, not only to scientists but to philosophers and theologians as well. In the first place, we don't like it when things go against our understanding of the way things work; the unpredictability implied by such events makes us feel unsteady on our feet. Besides, the notion that the Creator would interfere with the laws of his own Creation is unsettling. It might suggest that the Creation wasn't put together properly in the first place, so needs some tinkering. Or, the Creator himself might be suffering from the same whimsical tyranny exhibited by all those old pagan gods he was supposed to replace.

Above: *The miraculousness of nature is captured in this painting by D. Frankcom called* Musa paradisiaca *or banana with flower and butterfly,* (1703).

The Impossible...

It was perhaps an effort to come to terms with this discomfort that provoked St. Augustine to suggest that miracles are not contrary to *the laws of nature, but rather to our* understanding of *them. In that, he would appear to agree both with the Christian Scientists and with some of the modern-day investigators of the supernatural — and his statement reveals the profound influence the ancient Greeks had on his thinking, and indeed on the thinking of many of the early Christians.*

Thomas Aquinas, however, lived later on, in the thirteenth century when modern science was just beginning to stir in the womb of the Christian West. Eight centuries after Augustine, Aquinas was compelled to point out that such a definition held inherent dangers in the face of the expansion of scientific understanding. He noted that our ancestors considered an eclipse of the sun to be a sign of God's displeasure before science came along and explained that it was an effect of the moon passing between the earth and the sun. So he proposed that the causes of miracles must be *completely* hidden, and "wondrous in an unqualified way...*of itself filled with admirable wonder*, not simply in relation to one person or another."

In his *Summa Contra Gentiles*, Aquinas goes on to define a hierarchy of miracles, the highest being those which nature could never do (such as the sun standing still in aid of Joshua's battle against Jericho, or the parting of the Red Sea for the benefit of the fleeing Israelites) and at the next level those which nature can do, but not in the sequence in which they happen in the particular case. Creatures live, for example, but not *after* they have died; people can see, but not after they have been blind (an example it was possible to use so loosely only before the psychosomatic condition called hysteria became known).

He also allowed that miracles might happen even *in accordance with* the laws of Nature, as long as it could be established that she was not the responsible agent in this instance. In other words, people might naturally recover from illness, but in order to qualify as a miracle this recovery must be on account of God rather than the natural capacity of the body to heal itself.

Which brings us to the next, and perhaps most important element of the definition of miracles.

Right: Il Trionfo di San Tommaso d'Aquino. *St. Thomas Aquinas who wrote extensively about the different hierarchies of miracles is shown here in this sixteenth-century painting by Francesco Traini.*

The Divine...

Above: *This monument in St. Peter's Basilica in Rome was erected to Benedict XIV, who as Cardinal Prospero Lambertini, had served as a Devil's Advocate in determining who were genuine cases for canonization.*

The operative definition of miracles according to the Roman Catholic Church has remained essentially unchanged since it was written by Pope Benedict XIV (1675-1758) in his treatise, De Miraculus. By this time, countless miraculous abilities had been demonstrated by saints, and countless miraculous healings brought about by contact with the relics of saints and martyrs, or in response to prayers addressed to them.

Any definitive statement on miracles by the Church had to take into account all these wonders, and so Benedict allowed that miracle-working was not always a direct act of God, but could be delegated by him to angels and even to very pious men and women.

This does not mean that Benedict was "soft" on the question of miracles. On the contrary, as Cardinal Prospero Lambertini he had served as a "Devil's Advocate" (an actual term used in the process of canonization within the Vatican) in canonization proceedings for saints, and as such it was his job to challenge every report of the miraculous with all the reason, skepticism and science at his disposal. He was certainly well aware of what his younger contemporary, the Scottish philosopher David Hume, called "the strong propensity of mankind to the extraordinary and the marvelous."

Unlike Hume—whose *Enquiry Concerning Human Understanding* offered an argument against the probability of miracles so persuasive that theologians still feel compelled to counter it today—Lambertini/Benedict's faith in miracles was so strong that he was determined to sort out the true phenomena from the false ones once and for all. Benedict argued that miracles were not *contrary* to nature but *beyond* it, thus affirming that they were not just arbitrary spectacles of a whimsical God with no purpose other than to demonstrate his power to disrupt his own Creation. Just because something was extraordinary and impossible according to the laws of nature did not necessarily mean that it was divine—the event could be a result of sorcery or magic, and thus diabolical. Real miracles should "serve to confirm the Catholic Faith," he said, "or to demonstrate the sanctity of some man." They might be in answer to prayer, or to symbolize some aspect of God's teaching.

Thus we arrive at the core of the definition of miracles, which is that they must have some *significance* that can be identified as "divine." In

fact, the word used in John's Gospel to describe the miracles of Jesus was the Greek *semeion*, meaning "sign." Miracles are not just *thauma* — wonders that might be produced by any magician — but *signs* intended to convey a divine message through a concrete demonstration that those present are able to witness firsthand.

Various sects of Christianity might disagree about the miraculousness of a given event, but when they do they are really disagreeing about the definition of God, not the definition of the miraculous. The Pope believes in a Catholic God, who conveys his will through the Councils of the Church. Those Councils have shaped Roman Catholic doctrine over the centuries, and have declared that speaking in tongues, for example, is not generally something God uses as a "sign." Pentecostal Christians, on the other hand, believe the ability to speak in tongues, to handle poisonous snakes, or to be impervious to fire, for example, is a fulfillment of Christ's promise in Acts 1:8 when he said, "You shall receive power when the Holy Spirit has come upon you; and you shall be my witnesses...to the end of the earth." The two sects disagree not on the fundamental proposition that a miracle is a "sign" from God, but rather on what sort of entity this God is—and, as a consequence, what events he considers appropriate to use in "signaling" his people.

A Question of Faith

If it were left to the theologians and philosophers, the debate about what specific events should be classified as miracles could go on for eternity. Certainly it has been going on at least since New Testament times, and it continues today.

But in the last analysis miracles are not just events "out there" that can be measured and debated and proved. They are also events witnessed by an audience, and their effect is to provoke in that audience a sense of wonder, awe, or transcendent understanding. Miracles, in other words, provoke or strengthen "faith" in those who witness them.

Faith, as H. L. Mencken so aptly put it, is "an illogical belief in the improbable." Does that mean that faith equals superstition and delusion, as so many sceptics would claim? No, not necessarily. At its best, an "illogical belief in the improbable" is not so much a "belief" as a knowing, based on personal experience. It is illogical not because it is untrue, but because the truths which it encounters—love, beauty, grace, compassion, transcendence—fall outside the rightful province of the logical mind. To bring logic to love is to destroy it, to insist on the improbability of beauty is to pull a veil over our own eyes and complain that the world has grown ugly. To say that because the stirrings of the human spirit cannot be measured in a laboratory it means they are not real, is to deny meaning to human existence.

The Protestant theologian Paul Tillich has said, "Revelation belongs to a dimension of reality for which scientific and historical analysis are inadequate. Revelation is the manifestation of the depth of reason and the ground of being. It points to the mystery of existence and to our own

...suddenly there came a sound from heaven as of a rushing mighty wind, and it filled all the house where they were sitting. And there appeared unto them cloven tongues like as of fire, and it lay upon each of them. And they were all filled with the Holy Spirit, and began to speak with other tongues, as the spirit gave them utterance.

(ACTS 2 : 2-4)

Above: Pentecoste *by Tiziano*.

Above: *The ascension of Jesus to heaven, an event that is crucial to the faith of Christians, is depicted in this painting* l'Ascensione *by Andrea Mantegna (1431-1506).*

The miracle of St. Nicholas

The peculiarity of some saints has also been shown in their extraordinary and often precocious maturity. The concept of the *puer senex*, or aged child, is popular in hagiographical studies. Some cried from inside the womb, and stood immediately after birth, while others jumped enthusiastically into the baptismal font and dipped themselves in holy water. Babies learned to write within three days of birth, were born with monastic tonsures, or wobbled off to monasteries within moments of learning to walk. Saint Nicholas is said to have begun his fasting while still on the breast, refusing to suckle except on Wednesdays and Fridays!

ultimate concern." The primary function of miracles is not to shock the senses, but to bring revelation—to grant us a glimpse of the divine and, through that glimpse, the opportunity to be transformed. Tillich even argues that there are no such things as "objective" miracles. The subjective wonder and ecstasy of the beholder, he says, is so intrinsic to the miracle that the miraculous can be said truly not to exist outside the moment in which it is experienced.

"Beholding the glory of the Lord," said Saint Paul, "we are ourselves changed from one degree of glory to another." Thus the true meaning of faith—and the fundamental meaning of the miraculous—is to be found not in the narrowing exercise of following dogmas and reciting catechisms, but in acquiring the trust and courage to go beyond mere belief into the uncharted territory of knowing. It is to allow ourselves to go beyond our own self-imposed limitations and enter a realm where miracles are possible.

A Few Notes About Miracle Country

Faced with the whole of miracle history, the first challenge is how to go about presenting its cornucopia of wondrous ingredients. There are miracles of healing and miracles of destruction, miracles performed by God and those enacted by his angelic or human representatives. The passage of time seems to have affected both the kinds of miracles that happen and the ways in which we have interpreted their meaning. A variety of "maps" have been offered, from Thomas Aquinas' three-tiered hierarchy to the contemporary psychical researchers' categories of clairvoyance, psychokinesis, and so on.

C. S. Lewis speaks of two broad categories which he calls "Miracles of the Old Creation" and "Miracles of the New Creation." Miracles of the Old Creation, he says, are those in which something that normally happens in accordance with natural law, following the accepted timetables and rules, is enacted by God in a local and immediate way. In this sense, the miracle is in some way quantitative rather than strictly qualitative. Water, through the agency of vines, soil, and sun, becomes wine. A small amount of "bread," through the agency of seed, is planted and becomes more bread. When Jesus turns water into wine at the wedding feast, or feeds five thousand people with five loaves of bread, he is not going against the laws of nature as we understand them, but only enacting them in a miraculous way. Among the Miracles of the Old Creation, Lewis counts these two examples of "fertility" miracles along with healings, Jesus' one act of destruction in withering the fig tree, and some of a fourth category that he calls "miracles of dominion over the inorganic," like the stilling of the tempest.

Right: This beautiful ceiling from the Sala del mappamondo fresco by G. De Vecchi and da Reggio shows the constellations of the twelve signs of the Zodiac. Mankind's fascination with his environment has led him into investigations of the complex laws of nature, through such disciplines as astronomy, in order to understand the world in which he lives.

The more startling miracles of "dominion over the inorganic," typified by Jesus' act of walking on water, are Miracles of the New Creation. In Lewis' scheme these types of miracles also include those of "reversal" of nature's laws, like raising the dead, and "miracles of perfecting or glorification" such as Christ's resurrection and ascension.

In a Miracle of the New Creation, it is the happening itself which is miraculous, and not just its timing and circumstance. These are the miracles which, in Lewis' words, provide "the foretaste of a Nature that is in the future"—a future which is, to varying degrees in virtually all religions, characterized by the restoration of humanity to its home in Paradise. In most of the Eastern religions this restoration is seen as purely a spiritual one, as the individual consciousness merges once again with the Absolute. The Judeo-Christian tradition anticipates the reunion in a future Judgment Day when not only the spirit but also the individual "spirit body"—and in the views of some Christians the whole of Nature herself—will be admitted to the Kingdom of God.

Lewis excuses himself from the task of categorizing the Old Testament miracles by saying that in his view the Old Testament contains at least as much mythology as history, and by claiming both lack of sufficient expertise and asserting the necessity to limit the scope of his book to the New Testament. He does express the view that "Myth in general is not merely misunderstood history… nor diabolical illusion… nor priestly lying… but, at its best, a real though unfocused gleam of divine truth falling on human imagination." It is in this context that some of the Old Testament miracles will be examined in the pages to follow. The purpose will be neither to assert nor to deny their historical reality, but rather to shed some light on the common functions of myth and miracle in symbolizing the human encounter with the divine.

Finally, there are a few countries on the map of the miraculous which were either excluded by Lewis by his own choice, or have arisen in the half-century since his book was written. Nowadays the miracle landscape includes many commentaries,

Left: *Many religions believe in an afterlife where the efforts of this world will be rewarded. Here is an image which depicts the Islamic view of Paradise as promised to the faithful.*

interpretations, and lookout points which, though by no means orthodox, are nevertheless deeply rooted in the assumptions and belief systems of the Judeo-Christian West. These include everything from *A Course in Miracles* to channeled messages from deep space, and in this book will be grouped under the general heading of Miracles for a New Millennium.

With this map in hand, then, it is time to set out on a tour of the impossible, the extraordinary, and the divine.

Right: The Fall of Jericho *by Jean Fouquet (c. 1425-1480) is a medieval painting depicting the victorious army after the city's fall.*

Part Two
The Foundations of the Miraculous

Bishop Ambrose of Milan went into a trance as he knelt at the altar and, to the astonishment of the congregation, remained motionless for two or three hours. When he came out of it, he explained that St Martin of Tours had died, and he had been at the funeral, he then carried on the service from the point where he left off. When it was found that St Martin's funeral had taken place at the time, and as described, this could be held to have been a divine dispensation to Ambrose.

What we now know as the Christian Bible was written over hundreds of years, by a succession of different cultures, in the languages of Hebrew, Aramaic and Greek. The various writings that make up the New Testament were not created until after the death of Jesus, during a period most scholars have fixed from A.D. 50 to 115. The Old Testament is a collection of writings which include oral traditions, historical accounts, and scriptures sacred to the Jews among whom Jesus was born.

During the first century of Christianity, the new Christians continued to use the existing Jewish scriptures—there was, at first, no distinctively Christian canon, nor apparently any perceived need for one. The appearance of Jesus as the Messiah prophesied in the Jewish scriptures was sufficient unto itself as a basis for the new religion, and the first preoccupation of the Apostles was to spread this news.

By the second century, however, the new Church had begun to set aside specifically Christian writings and to treat them as equal to the existing Jewish scriptures. Thus the distinction between "New" and "Old" Testaments was born, and—despite an attempt by Marcion in the second century to exclude the Old Testament books altogether—the two collections were eventually combined. A few variations remain in the scriptures of different sects, but by and large the whole collection of writings became the Holy Bible of Christians.

The Jews had always believed that scripture was

Above: *This image of St. Martin of Tours is taken from the* Book of Hours, *a French medieval manuscript.*

meant to be a living entity, an inexhaustible mine of wisdom whose truths were eternal—written in ancient times, perhaps, but at the same time comprehensible to each new generation by means of exegesis, or "translating" and interpreting words and events that otherwise would seem to apply to a time long past. It is in this sense that many of the Old Testament writings are considered to be "mythological," to the extent that they cannot be taken at face value but must be mined for the "gleam of divine truth" that lies hidden within them. Only in that way can their meaning for the present be understood. The Church Fathers followed this tradition of exegesis in the early centuries of Christianity by reinterpreting much of the Old Testament in light of the teachings of Jesus. So Christians today do not practice animal sacrifice, for example, but might interpret the Old Testament scriptures concerning these rituals to fit a contemporary ideal of reverence for life and gratefulness to God for providing food. The miracle stories of the Bible, too, have been interpreted differently depending on whether the interpreters consider them to be actual, historical events, or allegorical representations of sacred teachings — or, in some cases, both.

Right: *The Garden of Eden, believed to be real by fundamentalists, has also been interpreted as a reflection of a paradisiacal past that can be seen in many mythologies. This painting,* Paradiso terrestre *by Jan il Vecchio Bruegel, shows his interpretation of that idyllic past.*

In the Beginning...

In the beginning God created the heaven and the earth. And the earth was without form, and void; and darkness was upon the face of the deep. And the Spirit of God moved upon the face of the waters. And God said, Let there be light: and there was light. GENESIS 11-3

The first miracle was, of course, Creation itself. Most scientists now—with the notable exception of Steven Hawking (author of *A Brief History of Time)* — subscribe to the theory that the universe began with a "Big Bang," which happened approximately fifteen billion years ago. From this "pure potential" exploded all the "actual" that makes up the present universe. This idea, like all the other Holy Grails of science that remain just slightly out of reach, is supported by some scientific observations and troubled by others. For now, it is the "working hypothesis" to which the majority of scientists subscribe.

Another, related idea, has been put forward by astrophysicist John Gribbin. He proposes that this first Big Bang has been followed by others, that in fact the universe is in a sense an "evolving" organism on a grand scale. To explain it perhaps over-simply: Some stars called "supernovas," when they seem to be self-destructing by consuming themselves in their own furnaces, eventually end up collapsing to form

what is known as a "black hole." According to current scientific understanding, the black hole has such powerful gravitational force that nothing can escape from it, including light. But, says Gribbin, that truth only applies to our universe. There is nothing to prevent the "stuff" gathered into this black hole from erupting into another dimension. In other words, when a star in our universe dies in this way, it creates another Big Bang, and thereby another universe, in another dimension.

To the question of where it all began, then, Gribbin answers, in the death of a star in another universe, in another dimension. Hawking, on the other hand, asserts that the universe had no beginning, nor will it have an end. In reality, since time is an invention of the human mind, there are four dimensions of space—and if this is true, the universe is both self-contained and limitless.

Hindus say that there are innumerable worlds comparable to our own, each containing "finer" worlds above, and "coarser" worlds below, and each issuing from the same source. "Just as the spider pours forth its thread from itself and takes it back again, even so the universe grows from the

Left: *This beautiful photograph captures the initial stages of a spider spinning its web in the early morning, when the dew still clings to the trees.*

Imperishable," say the Upanishads. Following the analogy, when the spider withdraws the thread, which it does from time to time, the cosmos collapses into a "Night of Brahma" and all that has been manifested in the phenomenal world is returned to the source, as pure potentiality. The universe "breathes" in this way, into being, back into nonbeing, and into being again. And in their view that it has been doing so for ever — no beginning, no end — the Hindus seem, in some odd way, to reconcile the views of Hawking and Gribbin. But even the Hindus feel the need to have Brahma behind the whole affair, and in the Judeo-Christian tradition, that's where the idea of God comes in.

The revolutionary contribution made by the Genesis story, commonly believed to have been written down by a priest who lived in the sixth century B.C., was to introduce "law" and coherence into a world that had previously been ruled by the power struggles and whims of a whole pantheon of gods.

Right: *Creation myths from various cultures often have common threads. Although Hindu mythology attributes its ultimate creative power to Brahma, it nevertheless views the world as having no beginning or end, a view that is very compatible to certain modern scientific theories. In this painting, through the churning of the sea milk, Vishnu plans cosmic order by causing demons and gods to pull Sesha, the cosmic serpent.*

Other Near Eastern creation myths at the time spoke of a divine struggle to subdue a willful and recalcitrant primordial matter. Genesis introduced a single God who had both the power to create the universe without opposition, and the life-affirmative sentiments to pronounce his creation "good." Furthermore, he created the Garden of Eden not as a special place in the heavens set aside for the gods, but as a landscape on Earth specifically designed to provide for all the needs of human beings.

From the beginning he seems to have granted freedom of choice to these humans he created in his own image—it was he who told them about the Tree of Knowledge in the first place, and presumably placed it in the Garden as a test of some sort. Obviously, they had at least enough freedom to be disobedient, to sacrifice the "faith" of their innocent dependence on God and thrust themselves into a world "east of Eden" where they had to struggle for a living, experience pain in childbirth, and eventually die and return to the dust whence they had come. But even in his apparent wrath God looks after his human creatures, giving them proper clothing to replace the fig leaves they have used, thanks to their newly-acquired knowledgeability, to cover their nakedness. Thus attired, they are expelled from a Garden where everything had been miraculous, and therefore taken for granted, into a landscape where from now on, the miraculous would be their only reminder of their Creator's continuing concern.

The Miracle of Life

Most of us are familiar with the idea that at one time in the distant past of planet Earth there was a "primordial soup," and into this soup came an initiatory zap of electricity from above, a "thunderbolt" of lightning, provoking this soup into a form of awakening life.

The problem with this idea, as scientists discovered in the 1950s, is that such an event would have provoked only simple organic compounds, not the infinitely complex and self-reproducing stuff of life known as DNA. In scientific terms, then, life is a "miracle." The medieval alchemists seem to have suspected as much, with their theories of a "secret ingredient" that was the key to transmuting base metals into gold, for example — or, as some of them claimed to be able to do, creating little holograms of life in laboratories.

Recent efforts to uncover the secrets of the miracle of life have led some scientists to invent a new field of exploration — complexity. Somehow, contrary to the second law of thermodynamics, all things do not move inexorably towards cooling off, chaos, and disintegration. In fact, quite the opposite seems to happen. Various species organize themselves into complex communities, societies, and ecosystems. And even "non-living" things like sand dunes seem

Above: *This painting,* Adam and Eve in the Garden of Eden, *by Lucas Cranach* (1472-1553) *shows the fall from grace when Eve decides to try the fruit from the Tree of Knowledge, which brings about their loss of innocence and expulsion from an earthly paradise.*

Above: *An example of fractal geometry. This is a computer graphics image derived from the Julia Set, a class of shapes plotted from complex number coordinates. Each point is assigned a color depending upon its behavior under a series of simple, but repeated, mathematical operations or mappings.*

to have a mind of their own, as they retain their essential shapes in their journeys across Middle Eastern deserts.

The new scientific explorers of complexity are on a search for the underlying elegance in all the teeming, unpredictable, yet somehow harmonious variety of life. Some of them have even tried to apply their new theories to the behavior of stock markets, apparently with impressive success. Their laboratories are often wholly within the software programs of computers, where they set up miniature worlds so they can watch them evolve on the screen. James Lovelock, the proponent of the Gaia hypothesis that views Earth as a living organism, has created "Daisyworld," for example—a place where differently-colored computer "plants" establish themselves on a computer "planet" in response to the availability of computer "sunlight." Once established, Lovelock can "play God" with the equilibrium of Daisyworld by, say, adjusting the solar energy available in an amount equivalent to that between the last ice age, and today. Daisyworld responds spectacularly, growing new varieties and establishing itself in new areas to celebrate the change. "A simple change produces a complex response," in other words. The breath of a butterfly in Mexico provokes a thunderstorm in England. "We are all related," says Black Elk of the Lakota.

Rupert Sheldrake, on the other hand, points out that "mathematics has been remarkably unsuccessful in dealing with biology and biological forms." To Sheldrake, the "language of God" when it comes to the creation of life is not spoken in the alphabet of mathematics and computer programs but in something he searches for words to describe as "some non-physical or trans-physical reality, spiritual in nature." Biologists like Sheldrake can't help but observe that in living systems, whether that be a human being or a bacterium, the whole is greater than the sum of its parts. His theory attempts a scientific explanation of the miraculous ways in which embryos develop, for example, and plants grow from seeds. Basically, he says, things develop in the way they do because there exists something called a "morphogenetic field" that defines and shapes the development of any particular form. It's almost as if something "grows into" a blueprint or mold that exists around it, even if we can't detect the blueprint with our senses.

Furthermore, the blueprint is reinforced by the existence of other, similar blueprints. Acorns grow into oak trees because generations of oaks have developed the habit of doing so, and the "morphogenetic field" is the official messenger of this habit to acorns everywhere. A bit of a developing embryo can be surgically removed, and it will regenerate itself to fill its blueprint, because the blueprint is there to fill. Rats in New Jersey can be taught to navigate through a maze, and their learning, conveyed through the "morphic resonance"

The miracle of Saint Gerald

The modesty of Saint Gerald of Aurillac prevented him from performing miracles directly, but the sick who lived within the range of his travels would steal the water he had washed in and use it to cure his ills. A lame child, it was reported, arranged with friends to acquire the water from Gerald's servants and sprinkled it on his useless legs, which immediately were able to carry the boy as any normal legs should.

of rathood, will enable successive generations of rats in California to learn the same task more quickly.

"If you start using psychological language," Sheldrake offers by way of clarification, "and you start talking in terms of thought, then you've got a handier way of thinking of the influence of the past [in creating the morphogenetic field] because with mental fields you have memory. And one can extend this memory, if one thinks of the whole universe as essentially thought-like...then you automatically have a sort of cosmic memory developing." He points out that this view is also held by Mahayana Buddhists—their idea of it is called the *alayavijnana,* or storehouse of consciousness — and even by the Theosophists in their notion of the *akashic* records, where everything that transpires, physical or mental, is recorded and serves as a sort of databank to back up the laws of karma.

So where does the "non-physical or trans-physical reality, spiritual in nature" come into Sheldrake's theory? He describes a "nesting" of four levels of possibility that he feels are compatible with his hypothesis. The first is the material level, which he believes includes his morphogenetic fields. The second is the level of human consciousness, where for example new forms can arise from the activity of the mind and its creativity. The third is a similar consciousness that exists in the natural world, and can develop new forms of crystals, or varieties of

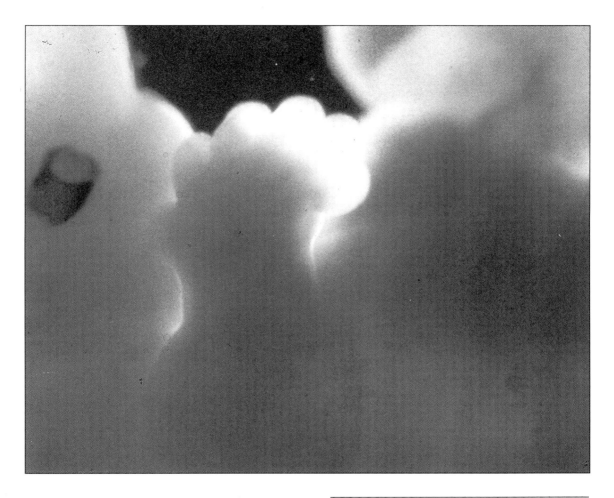

plants and so on. And finally, there is the source beyond all these: "This would correspond to the traditional theistic views of creation," he says, "which would have a God who is beyond, above, and in nature."

Above: *The human embryo at about 7-8 weeks, showing the head with the retina of the eye (dark spot) and the beginning of the nose visible; the developing arms, hands, and legs are visible on the left side of the body. The umbilicus, connecting the embryo with its mother's circulation is seen at the top left. This is no doubt one of nature's most profound miracles.*

Above: *For most societies, the appearance of the rainbow after the rain symbolizes luck and new beginnings.*

The Promise of the Rainbow

I do set my bow in the cloud, and it shall be for a token of a covenant between me and the earth. And it shall come to pass, when I bring a cloud over the earth, that the bow shall be seen in the cloud. And I will remember my covenant, which is between me and you and every living creature of all flesh; and the waters shall no more become a flood to destroy all flesh. GENESIS *9: 13-15*

At the end of Steven Spielberg's captivating movie *ET,* the spaceship which carries the little extraterrestrial back to his home paints a glowing, multicolored arc of light across the night sky.

It serves as both reassurance of good intentions and the promise of happy endings—and, in its biblical context, a promise never to destroy the Earth and all its creatures.

The rainbow remains one of the most powerfully wondrous sights for all of us, whenever it appears.

Who has not called friends and family to "look at the rainbow!"? Who has not on occasion felt, in that moment, the reassurance it brings that there is peace after every storm, a bright hope for every tomorrow. The rainbow has a special significance in mythologies of virtually every culture on the planet—in places as remote from one another as Japan, Australia, and Mesopotamia the rainbow has been seen as a reminder of the bridge that once connected heaven and earth and could be traveled by all. The rainbow is one of the most important "guardian spirits" of the Navajos in their healing rituals, and the drums of shamans in central Asia are decorated with rainbows representing their journeys to the Otherworld.

While the Creation story of Genesis reveals a God who has sovereign power over the universe and takes a personal interest in his creation, the story of Noah's Ark and the flood reveals that he can also use his powers to destroy. In the biblical story, as in other, similar myths of the Near East and many other places around the world, the flood was a divine purification of a world gone drastically wrong. In cleansing the earth, the God of the Bible chooses one righteous man, Noah, and his family to survive and start the world over again, having also safeguarded sufficient pairs of the rest of Earth's creatures to put it back together as it had been. In allowing his creation to flourish once more, the warrior-god "hangs up his bow" and gives the world a second chance.

Many biblical scholars compare this story in Genesis with the subsequent story of God's parting the waters of the Red Sea to help the Israelites escape Egyptian slavery. In the epic tale of Exodus, God again uses his power over nature to drown the bad and save the good. But, in keeping with his promise symbolized by the rainbow, this catastrophe is local and specific, not a worldwide cataclysm. The details of how this was accomplished, however, appear to have been derived from a more ancient Near Eastern mythology of a divine encounter with a sea dragon in which the cleaving of the monster in two by the deity delivered the people from slavery.

The earliest account of the Israelites' fortuitous escape from the Egyptians is believed to be the "song

Right: *The rainbow of the ark symbolizes a man's second chance to rebuild life on earth in accordance with God's laws. The myth of a great flood that destroys the earth before purifying it is present in many mythologies of the Far East.*

of Moses" recorded in Exodus 15. This song suggests something more on the order of a sudden, divinely instigated storm than the supernatural act so stunningly depicted by Cecil B. De Mille in his movie, *The Ten Commandments*. It has been suggested that by the time the priestly author of Exodus committed the story to writing, the historical legend of the Israelites' escape had been thoroughly mixed up with the ancient dragon-splitting myth, no doubt because the story was more appealing that way.

In fact the earlier version is more believable: the Red Sea, or Sea of Reeds is, as its name suggests, a marshy location where the Israelites might well have been able to find a dry pathway across. A well-timed storm, divinely directed or not, might well have caused the pursuing Egyptians to get bogged down in the wrong place, and even to drown. In either case, the point is the same: God's people can rely on him for help in even the most impossible situations and, just as it happened in *ET*, to deliver them from slavery and death in a thrilling, last-minute rescue.

Left: *This fourteenth-century Italian fresco shows Moses and the Israelites crossing the Red Sea. Moses performed this miracle, the parting of the sea, in order to lead God's chosen people from exile into freedom.*

Above: *Mount Ararat has been the site of many 'arkeological' expeditions. This engraving shows the Ark beaching on the crest of Mount Ararat.*

The Miraculous as History

In 1829, an explorer named Friedrich Parrot broke an ancient taboo, long honored by the region's inhabitants, and led an expedition up the slopes of Mount Ararat in Armenia. Here, according to Genesis, was where Noah's Ark came to rest after the great flood. Parrot was not looking for the ark, nor did he find it. But many who followed him did find something that at least seemed to them to be the remains of the great ship that God ordered Noah to build.

Among the first was an archdeacon of Chaldaea named Nouri, who scaled Ararat in the company of several other people and found the ark whole and definitely recognizable. He was "almost overcome" with gratitude, he said, not for his own sake—he had never been in any doubt that the scriptures represented historical truth—but for the sake of the unbelievers who would now be persuaded to convert to Christianity.

In later years Charles Fort, the intrepid American investigator of all things paranormal, was not impressed. "I accept," he commented dryly, "that anybody who is convinced that there are relics upon Mount Ararat has only to climb up Mount Ararat, and he must find something that can be said to be part of Noah's Ark." But Nouri's expedition was followed by many others, and many have brought back pieces of what appear to be crafted timber from the icy mountaintop. In the twentieth century, pilots flying over the area have spotted "arkeological" remains on more than one occasion. Most of these alleged relics of the ark have been put aside for lack of sufficient scientific evidence of their authenticity, and seem to fall into that category of miraculous discoveries described by Fort: those which take place when people find what they expect or hope to find.

The legend of the great flood, and the survival of Noah, his family, and all the earth's creatures inside the ark, remains one of the most popular and well-known miracle stories of the Old Testament. This great drama in Genesis is also strikingly similar to an earlier Mesopotamian legend in which the hero Xisuthros is warned by the god Cronus to build a ship to escape a coming deluge. He does so, and after the deluge he, like Noah, releases birds in order to determine if the floodwaters have begun to recede.

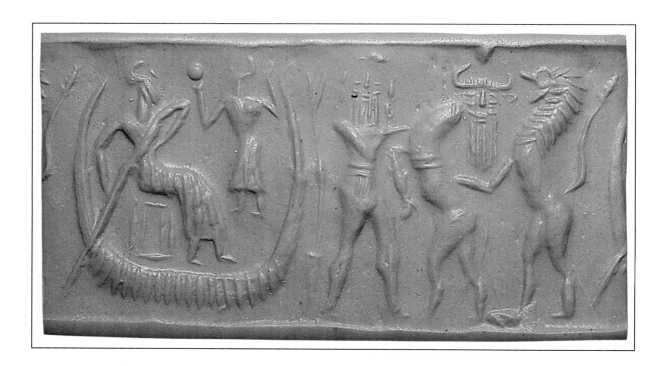

Above: *This flood epic engraving shows Utanapishtim in the ark and Gilgamesh fighting the bull. There are many similarities in this myth to that of Noah's story.*

Both these Middle Eastern legends in turn share an extraordinary number of features with many other stories from diverse cultures around the world. In Hindu mythology, for example, Manu—a kind of Hindu "Adam" who keeps reappearing at the beginning of the various ages of humankind—is ordered by Vishnu in the guise of a fish to build a ship so that he can survive a great flood. In one version of the story he is instructed, like Noah, to take with him in the boat the "essences and seeds of all living creatures" to protect them from destruction. In the nineteenth century, a collection of ancient Sumerian writings were rediscovered in which the hero is Gilgamesh, a king who lived about 2700 B.C. In this legend, Gilgamesh meets Utanapishtim, human-turned-immortal and the only survivor of a great flood who had been warned by one of the gods of the impending deluge so that he could save himself. Utanapishtim, furthermore, saved not only himself and his immediate family, along with the animals, but also a number of skilled craftsmen. His ship came to rest on the mountain of Nisir, and he released a dove and then a swallow, who both came back without finding a place to land. When the third bird, a raven, failed to return, Utanapishtim knew the flood must be receding. Farther north, in similarly ancient times, Deucalion and his wife Pyrrha, Greek survivors of a worldwide deluge, came to rest on the top of Mount Parnassus and repopulated the Earth by throwing stones on the ground which sprang to life as human beings.

In fact, there are so many myths mentioning a "great flood" that one is tempted to believe that such a cataclysm must have occurred, wiping out most of the known world and forcing what was left of the human race to start over again in a dramatically altered landscape. Earlier in this century, the archeologist Sir Leonard Woolley came to the conclusion that an extraordinary flood must have occurred over most of Lower Mesopotamia around 3000 B.C.

Above: *This Islamic manuscript that dates from 1583 depicts Jonah and the whale and the prophet Jeremiah.*

God's Miraculous Messengers

I will raise them up a Prophet from among their brethren… and will put my words into his mouth; and he shall speak unto them all that I shall command him.
[DEUTERONOMY 18:18]

Jonah, says the Bible, was one day commanded by God to go and "cry against" the sinful city of Nineveh. But for some reason he decided to refuse his commission, instead setting out on a boat in the opposite direction. God was not pleased and unleashed a storm which threatened to break the boat to pieces. Despite the best efforts of the crew to spare both Jonah and themselves, God wouldn't stop the tempest until the disobedient prophet had been cast into the sea. There he was promptly swallowed up by "a great fish" that had been divinely prepared for the job. "And Jonah was in the belly of the fish three days and three nights." (Jonah 1:17)

Generations of young children, not to mention adults, who have heard this popular Old Testament story have been troubled by its outlandish assertions. One might accept that God speaks to people, causes storms, and all manner of other unlikely things, but

that somebody could actually survive inside the belly of a fish for three days is perhaps pushing reality too far? Perhaps it is not meant to be taken literally. Perhaps it is some kind of allegory, and if so, then what is the point of the story?

"God can do anything he likes," declares the Bible literalist. "And if you're thinking of disobeying Him you should keep that in mind. *That* is the point of the story." It is the sort of attitude that can threaten a Galileo with excommunication for his observation that the earth moves around the sun, or threaten a school teacher with imprisonment for teaching Darwin's theory of evolution: God can do whatever he likes. He can put 36,000-year-old skeletons in the ground to test our faith, or he can allow the devil to work through a scientist. The fact that he can do all these things is what makes him God. Argument finished.

It is an argument which has begun to lose some of its bite in the past two centuries. Now there are countless theologians and Bible scholars who are willing to discuss the mythological underpinnings of the story of Jonah and the Whale, and even to admit the possibility that Jesus appeared to his disciples after the crucifixion not as a physical entity but as a spiritual Being of Light. Shamans in many primitive cultures, we are told by anthropologists, share in common an initiatory experience often symbolized by being carried by an animal into the underworld, or "dying" and being "reborn." To point this out, and to make the obvious comparisons, is no longer sufficient grounds for excommunication or imprisonment. The story of Jonah and the Whale is now generally believed to be a work of conscious fiction.

Then what is it doing in the Bible? It is there precisely because it is an initiation tale, and one which provides plenty of rich material for comparison with other initiatory adventures throughout the Bible. In it, we find themes that are repeated time and again when God "chooses" somebody to be his personal representative—the initial reluctance, the period of isolation, and the need to perform miracles in order to be believed, are just a few examples.

Much of the miracle and magic in the Old Testament belongs to God himself. He is the one who causes floods to cover the earth, who rains down fire and brimstone on Sodom and Gomorrah, who sends

Right: *A Tlingit shaman's mask from Yakutat, Alaska (1886). The shamans of many tribes throughout the world undertook initiatory journeys that mirror the experiences of many of the prophets of the Old Testament.*

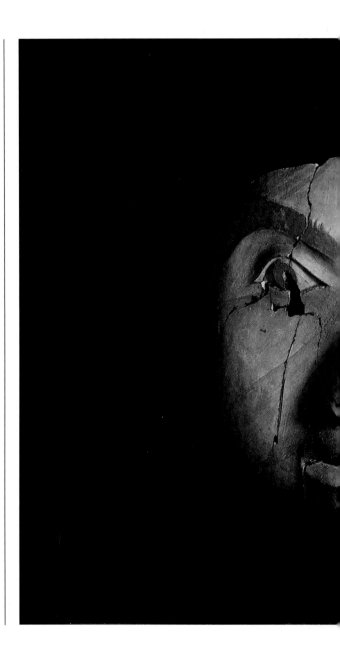

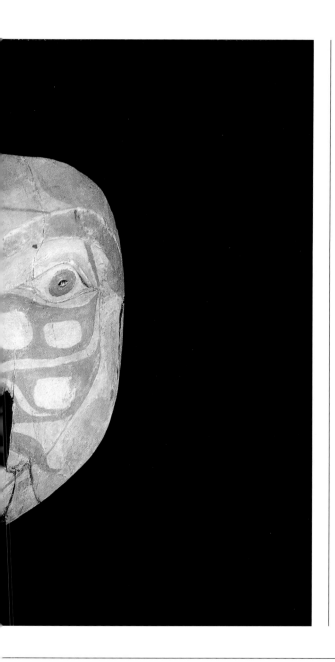

The miracle of Saint Catherine of Siena

Saints are also known to have the ultimate healing power—the ability to bring the dead back to life. One curious instance of this is reported in the life of Saint Catherine of Siena. When she learned that a woman had died without receiving the sacraments, Saint Catherine remained by the side of the body, swearing that she would not move until the woman returned to life. The miracle transpired very quickly.

Above: *This mosaic depicts Moses on Mount Sinai receiving his prophetic mission.*

plagues across Egypt to punish its transgressions against the Israelites, and who "hardens Pharaoh's heart" so that despite these plagues he won't free the Israelites from slavery. But this rather volatile warrior-god must also be given credit for the fact that on the occasions when he wasn't just trying to demonstrate his power, he generally tried to warn people ahead of time and give them a chance to change their sinful and disobedient ways.

If people had been able to listen to God directly, of course, they wouldn't have been misbehaving in the first place. Because they didn't listen, or perhaps didn't know how to listen, God needed human messengers who could get their attention and speak their language. Thus he found a few good men with spiritual potential, and dubbed them prophets. His instructions in Deuteronomy furthermore made it very clear that these prophets were not to be confused with the diviners, enchanters, witches and necromancers of the times. The test of authenticity was whether their prophecies came to pass: if they did, they belonged to God; if not, they were in somebody else's service.

Often, like Jonah, God's Old Testament prophets were reluctant to accept the assignment. The prophetic mission was no more socially acceptable in biblical times than it is today, and was often considerably more hazardous to life and limb. Even when the chosen prophet had courage enough to face the disbelieving masses, he often didn't feel worthy of the task. Moses, for example, argued that "I am not eloquent... I am slow of speech, and of a slow tongue." But God wasn't taking any excuses, and empowered Moses with miraculous tools so he could impress people enough to make them listen. The speaking duties were given to Moses' brother Aaron, and the rest is history according to Exodus, Leviticus, Numbers and Deuteronomy. It is a long and troubled history — God did not appear to be a very nice guy in those days, and was continually threatening people, testing them, and causing them no small amount of suffering. Not once, however, did Moses perform any miracles or deliver any messages without God's prior direction. The power was not in his human hands.

Joshua succeeded Moses, and the miracles of his leadership echo many of those which God had performed through his predecessor. The parting of the Red Sea became the parting of Jordan's waters, and Joshua was bidden to remove his shoes as he stood on holy ground before an angel, just as Moses had been commanded as he stood before the burning bush. God-sent hailstones fell on the Amorites as they had done on the Egyptians, and Joshua's magical spear performed wonders similar to those wrought by Moses' magical rod. But Joshua's task was essentially that of a warrior, and his most famous miracles are connected to the battles he led at God's command. The walls of Jericho were toppled by an elaborate ritual involving circling the city seven times, and blowing seven trumpets accompanied by great shouts from an army who had practiced silence for days beforehand. In another battle the sun "stood still in the midst of heaven, and hasted not to go down about a whole day." This, as the narrator of Joshua's story notes, was unusual in that God stopped the sun in response to Joshua's request rather than the other way around: "And there was no day like that before or after it, that the Lord hearkened unto the voice of a man."

Not all the miraculous powers bestowed by God were of such catastrophic import. Solomon, when God appeared to him in a dream and asked what he would like as a reward for being such a good man, replied simply that he wanted a wise and understanding heart so that he could administer to the needs of the people. "I am but a little child," said Solomon, in a touching display of innocence. "I know not how to go out or come in." His famous judgment regarding which of two women claiming the same child was the real mother is no less a "miracle" for being so simple and accessible to ordinary mortals.

The later prophets of the Old Testament begin to foreshadow the miracles of the New, and their stories feature more appearances of angels, miraculous healings, and predictions of the coming Messiah. But there were still plenty of fireworks to behold before John the Baptist—"a new Elijah"—appeared on the scene to baptize Jesus. The old Elijah, for example, bested the priests of a rival religion by igniting a sacrificial bull on the summit of Mount Carmel. After an illustrious prophetic career, he finally ascended to heaven in a chariot of fire, drawn by flaming horses. Elijah's successor Elisha performed miracles on the order of those later performed by Jesus, including healing a leper and bringing a dead child back to life. But it seems Elisha didn't "suffer the children" as gladly as Jesus; when a group of them teased him for being bald he cursed them and had them carried off by she-bears.

As the Old Testament stories progress through historical time, a number of features stand out as worthy of comment. One has been hinted at here, which is the recurrence of certain themes—the "magic wands," the crossing of waters, the healings, the days and nights spent in the wilderness, on mountaintops, in caves, in the belly of a great fish. Second is the almost universal reluctance of the chosen prophets to speak, so great are their feelings of unworthiness for

the task. There is a danger in having miraculous powers, or in speaking with the voice of God—and that is the danger of using these divine powers for one's own personal aggrandizement. In their reluctance to take on the task, the chosen ones are demonstrating their awareness of their own limitations and in doing so, proving that they have the humility needed for the task.

Another noteworthy feature of Old Testament miracles is a subtle and progressive shift in the agency of miraculous power, from God alone to man as an instrument of God. Certainly God himself did not order that Elisha's small tormentors should be carried off by bears—but Elisha, as a spokesperson and instrument of God's will, had the power to make it happen. The fact that he used this power in defense of his own rather petty concerns is unusual in the biblical context, but certainly not unheard of. The old mixes uneasily with the new in Elisha and the later prophets, but the new is definitely taking hold. Thus we are prepared, when Jesus enters the stage, for a completely new kind of human being— one who embodies God's message in a way qualitatively different from those who have come before him.

At the same time, though, the details of Jesus' life repeat many of the archetypal themes contained in the Old Testament. Does this mean, then, that the whole of the Bible—and, by inference, the scriptures of all religions—is just an elaborate allegory, a written record of oral mythologies which have no basis in historical fact? Not necessarily. The revelatory experience— the experience of illumination, of initiation into the mysteries, or whatever name is given to this extraordinary event in a person's life—seems to be, at root, the same no matter where or to whom it happens. That this experience can be accompanied by certain extraordinary physical manifestations is attested to all over the world. Whenever such

extraordinary events do happen, they seem to provoke the same inarticulate wonder, the same despair at the inadequacy of the tongue to express it. And in every instance, there is one miracle which must precede all other miracles to come—the initiation, the baptism, the anointing, must take place first, to clear away whatever remains of the personal, ego-centered goals of the new miracle-worker. Only after that can he or she truly be a channel for the divine.

Above: *The ascent of the prophet Elijah.*
After having fulfilled his prophetic mission, Elijah rides up to heaven in a chariot of fire.

Above: Joseph Smith, the founder of The Church of Jesus Christ of the Latter-day Saints claimed to have been directed by the angel Moroni to write the Book of Mormon.

Joseph Smith, A Latter-Day Moses

Joseph Smith, Jr. (1805-1844) was the son of poor Vermont farmers who, as a young man, struggled to decide which of the bickering churches in western New York where he lived was the right one to join. In answer to his prayers Smith received a vision in which God and Christ appeared to him in a pillar of light and told him not to choose any of the existing denominations because they were all wrong.

They promised him that he would be shown the true church in due time, and in September of 1823 Smith was visited by an angel who called himself Moroni. Moroni told him that Mormon, a descendant of the ancient Israelites, had written a true history of the Church on gold tablets and buried them in some nearby hills. Smith had been chosen to recover these tablets and translate them, but was not to do so until four years hence.

Smith eventually found the plates, and his translations of them formed The Book of Mormon, published in 1830. This, along with subsequent writings created with the help of divine revelation, formed the basis on which the Church of Jesus Christ of the Latter-day Saints, whose members are commonly called Mormons, was founded. Both Smith and his church were harassed and persecuted wherever they tried to settle, and he himself was arrested and jailed for treason in Illinois in 1844, where an angry mob managed to break in and assassinate him.

Above: Echelle de Jacob *by Marc Chagall. Many people receive visions during the dream state.*

Dreams —
A Doorway to the Beyond?

One of the most important characteristics of a prophet, and for that matter all human beings who serve as "instruments of God" is the ability to put aside personal agendas and commit wholly to God's service. Some of the biblical prophets received their visions in dreams. "God speaks to man in one way, and in two," says the Book of Job, "though man does not perceive it. In a dream, in a vision of the night, when deep sleep falls upon men, while they slumber in their beds, then He opens the ears of men."

In fact, the interest in dreams and what they have to tell us about a world beyond our immediate senses is as old as humankind. Homer spoke of two types of dreams, the "false" and the "true." Hippocrates believed dreams could tell us something about our illnesses and their causes. Both Heraclitus and Pythagoras believed that the soul was able to travel away from the body in sleep, just as it did at death, and to converse with higher beings in its travels. Mohammed received his initiatory visions, before being given the Koran, in a series of dreams in which he was conveyed to the center of the world, conversed with Abraham, Moses and Jesus, and was shown the hidden secrets of the universe.

Clearly, such a rich tradition surrounding dreams—and only a very few have been mentioned here—must point to a human experience much more profound than just an idle discharge of electrical impulses or, as Freud suggested, a kind of movie that shows us our repressed desires. In fact, many cultures have viewed dreams as equivalent to the waking visions of prophets and seers. Because most of us are not so sensitive, nor so lacking in self-centered ego, we cannot receive such visions in our normal waking state, but we can receive them when we "get out of the way" by going to sleep.

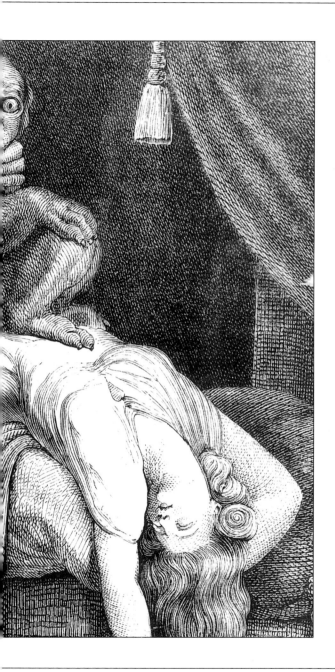

Left: *In the dream state many subconscious fears are released that in the ordinary waking state many people suppress. In this etching by Fuseli, we see some of the demons and strange creatures that can appear in our dreams and often symbolize hidden aspects of our subconscious.*

The Holy Shadow

Christianity is not the only religion to teach that miraculous powers contain their own dangers, and must not be sought directly.

One charming story, told in slightly different versions throughout almost all the Eastern traditions, is of a man who, because of his extraordinary goodness, was approached by God and offered the power to perform miracles. The man refused. "My life is so simple now," he said, "with so much beauty. So I cannot imagine, for one thing, that there could be anything more. And the second thing, this goodness that you say I possess is not my possession—in fact I am possessed by goodness, and goodness is doing its work without my interference. If you gave me the power to do miracles, you would be giving me a possession that I am doing perfectly well without. Indeed, I have renounced all possessions long ago. So please take your miraculous powers and give them to somebody else."

God argued with the man, of course, because the world was so much in need of miracles and there were so few good people who could be entrusted with the power to perform them. At last the man agreed, but only on one condition—that any miraculous happening should only take place behind his back, so that he never knew about it. In that way, he could be safe from the temptation to start to "possess" these powers, and thereby fall into the traps of self-importance and ego. The condition was agreed, and the miraculous powers were placed in the man's shadow. The story continues:

When he walked along, his shadow made arid paths green, caused withered plants to bloom, gave clear water to dried up brooks, fresh color to pale children, and joy to unhappy men and women. The man, meanwhile, simply went about his daily life, diffusing virtue as the stars diffuse light and the flowers scent, without being aware of it. The people, respecting his humility, followed him silently, never speaking to him about his miracles. Soon they even forgot his name, and called him "The Holy Shadow."

Above: Following the visions of the Virgin Mary at Fatima, Portugal, in 1917, this photograph shows the crowd in Cova da Iria who witnessed the 'Dance of the Sun' on October 13, 1917.

The "Dance of the Sun"

The more spectacular manifestations of divine ability to interfere with the laws of nature have been relatively scarce in recent times when compared with the tales told in the Old Testament. The closest parallels seem to have occurred mostly in connection with apparitions of the Virgin Mary and, perhaps most famously, in the events that took place early in this century in the village of Fatima, Portugal. Because of the possibility of various "psychic" phenomena operating to create Marian apparitions, the Roman Catholic Church has been very cautious in dispensing its blessings to such phenomena. Fatima is one of the few cases that have been recognized by the Church as a genuinely divine and miraculous happening.

As is the case in most Marian apparitions, the "chosen" visionaries at Fatima were children. Also typically, their world was one of political and social upheaval—World War One was raging through Europe, and the recently installed Portuguese government was openly hostile to the Catholic Church of which the children's families were devout members.

Nine-year-old Lucia dos Santos, and her friends Francesco and Jacinta Marto, aged eight and six respectively, were tending sheep in an area near their village known as the Cova da Iria when they all saw an "angel"—who appeared to be a boy of about fifteen—urging them to pray. In the weeks that followed he returned twice more with the same message, and then disappeared. Some months later, on May 13, 1917, the three children were again at the Cova when they were startled by a flash of lightning coming from a clear blue sky. They ran down the slope to safety, and there the two girls saw a beautiful, luminous woman standing within the foliage of a small oak tree. The boy Francesco could not see the apparition at first. But when he began to say the rosary, an instruction from the beautiful lady relayed by the girls, he too was able to share the vision although he could not hear her speak. The apparition requested that the children keep praying, and return to the spot on the thirteenth of every month for the following six months. She told them she was from heaven, and promised to reveal her full identity at the end of the six months.

Despite the fact that the children had agreed among themselves that they wouldn't tell anyone of their vision, Jacinta's excitement was too great to contain. She told her parents that she and the others had seen the Virgin Mary. Word soon spread, and the reaction of the village folk was about equally divided between scorn and reverence. The local priest was consulted, and he advised Jacinta's parents to allow her to keep her appointment the following month, but to discourage further visits if the child continued to report seeing an apparition. On June 13, the three children went to the Cova again, this time accompanied by about 50 local villagers. None of the crowd saw the "beautiful woman" but many did report seeing a "white cloud" rising from the oak tree at the time Lucia told them the apparition was leaving. Many observers also claimed that the branches of the tree were bent into a kind of "parasol" shape, which leaned towards the east as the cloud departed and remained in that position for several hours.

By July 13 the crowd of pilgrims had grown to 5000, and word of the phenomenon was beginning to spread throughout Portugal, causing no small amount of consternation in anti-clerical government circles.

The apparition continued to urge the children to tell people to pray for peace. Lucia asked that a miracle be performed so that the pilgrims could be convinced of the apparition's reality, and the lady agreed, saying that it would take place on October 13.

By August, government officials decided that the situation in Fatima was getting entirely out of hand.

Arthur d'Oliveira, a regional government official, was sent to the village to interrogate the children and force them to confess that they had been making the whole thing up. When they refused to recant, he went even further and took them to government facilities in a nearby city, where the interrogation grew more heavy-handed. He reportedly threatened the children with death, and told them individually that their playmates had already been executed for fraud and deception. Still, the children insisted on the truth of what they had seen, and were finally released. They had missed their August 13th apppointment, but even in their absence several thousand people had gathered in the Cova to see what would happen. At the appointed time, the assembled pilgrims heard what sounded like a loud explosion, saw a flash of lightning accompanied by rainbow-colored lights, and watched as a luminous cloud descended into the oak tree, lingered for a few seconds, and then went away.

In September, it became clear that the government's efforts to discredit the children had backfired. No less than thirty thousand people were present at Fatima on the 13th, where they were showered by white flower petals that miraculously appeared from the sky and disintegrated before they hit the ground. A government official, Antonio Robelo Martins, took a photograph of the miraculous rain and later published it in his book *Fatima Esperance du Mond.*

Above: This photograph shows the three children of Fatima to whom the Virgin Mary appeared. Fatima is now a site of pilgrimage by many thousands of devout Catholics.

The day of the promised October miracle saw about seventy thousand people coming to Fatima from all over the countryside. It was raining, and many of them had camped out overnight in the open in order to secure a place close to the oak tree. When the children arrived, took up their places near the tree and began to pray, the vision appeared to them again. The apparition finally revealed herself as Our Lady of the Rosary and asked that a chapel be built on the spot in her honor. After this conversation, suddenly Lucia cried out, "Look!" and as the crowd followed her eyes toward the sky they saw the clouds part to reveal a huge silver disc, rotating and throwing off colored flames. It remained in this position for about twelve minutes, turning the landscape into a wondrous and surreal tableau of rainbow-colored shadows. Most people assumed the disc was the sun. Suddenly, in the words of one observer, "a great cry, like a cry of anguish, arose from all this vast throng. The sun, while keeping its swiftness of rotation, detached itself from the firmament and, blood-red in color, rushed towards the earth, threatening to crush us."

The marvelous disc did not crush people, of course. But they did discover to their astonishment that once it had resumed its place in the sky and then disappeared, both their rain-soaked clothing and the sodden ground had dried.

A similar "dance of the sun" has been reported at Medjugorje in the former Yugoslavia, the site of a series of Marian apparitions witnessed by a group of

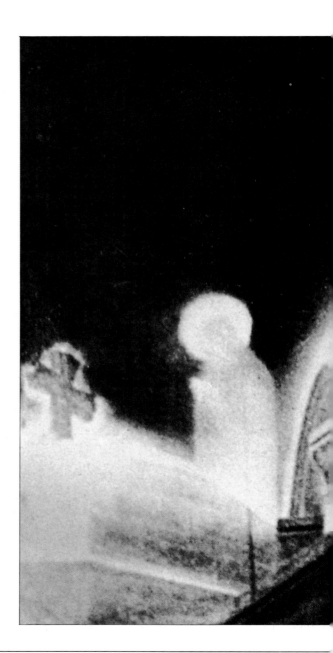

teenagers beginning in June, 1981. Among the witnesses of one such spectacular celestial display in 1986 were Mary Craig and Roger Stott, two reporters from the BBC. At the time, Craig allowed that what she had seen was indeed strange, but did not strike her in any way "numinous." The apparitions at Medjugorje continue as of this writing.

In both cases the children have been told "secrets" by the apparition which they are asked to reveal only under special circumstances. Lucia, who eventually joined a convent, finally told the secrets she had been given at Fatima, in response to a request from her superiors in the 1940s. One of these was that Jacinta and Francesco would die soon, which had indeed happened. The second was that if people continued in their ungodly behavior a great war would break out, preceded by a display of lights in the sky. Papers all over the world recorded the extraordinary displays of the Aurora Borealis in late January, 1938, shortly before the outbreak of the Second World War. The third has been kept secret by the Vatican, despite Lucia's indication that it could be released in 1960.

Left: The strange lights that appeared in 1968 around the Coptic Orthodox Church of St. Mary in Zeitoun, Cairo, Egypt, have been interpreted by witnesses as an apparition of the Virgin Mary.

"And the angel said unto her, Fear not, Mary: for thou hast found favor with God. And, behold, thou shalt conceive in thy womb, and bring forth a son, and shalt call his name JESUS."

(LUKE 1: 30-31)

Part Three
What Manner of Man is This?

The two specific events in the life of Jesus which are central to the Christian faith— and which must, more than any other of the miraculous phenomena associated with him, be "taken on faith"—are the virgin birth and the resurrection. The Immaculate Conception was not made a dogma of the Roman Catholic Church until Pope Pius IX declared it so in 1854, but it has long been felt that if one does not believe in the historical reality of these two miracles, one is not really a Catholic.

The implication—that Jesus is somehow a unique and "paranormal" phenomenon—has influenced the Western approach to the miraculous in ways both conscious and unconscious. Jesus was born miraculous, literally planted in his mother's womb by God. The rest of us are born in an ordinary way, and can therefore never expect to be able to exercise the same miraculous powers. He also, at least in one account, appeared physically after the crucifixion and made a point of insisting that he wasn't a ghost. The fact that nobody else has since been observed to do such a thing further testifies to his uniqueness.

Critiques of the miraculous aspects of Jesus' life have ranged from the sympathetic to the scornful, from the scholarly to the sensational. The New Testament itself gives plenty of scope for such disputes; there are striking differences to be found in the four Gospels, both in terms of the stories related and the context in which the stories appear. Neither Mark nor John, for example, even mention the specifics of Jesus' birth and childhood, and the earliest versions of

Above: *This tenth-century fresco depicts the Nativity. The Virgin Birth is considered a miracle by Christians; and an article of faith for Catholics.*

Opposite: *A detail of the face of Jesus from a painting by Cosimo Rosselli (1439-1507).*

Matthew in Hebrew do not include the first two chapters of the current version of that Gospel. Perhaps these authors were among those who, in the early days of Christianity, did not consider the story of the virgin birth to be central to the faith.

The scope of biblical scholarship has been expanded in recent years by the discoveries of the Dead Sea Scrolls, which have given clues to the historical and literary framework within which the Gospels were written and cleared up many questions about which passages had been added, altered, or taken away from them and when. The discovery of the so-called *Nag Hammadi* texts, which include the Gnostic gospels, has uncovered even more material that adds to our knowledge of the early development of Christianity and its scriptures. On one end of the spectrum, Jesus is portrayed as even more a concrete historical figure than the Church would allow. In her book *Jesus the Man*, for example, Dead Sea Scrolls scholar Barbara Thiering argues that Jesus was a member of a radical sect of the Essenes, engaged in a power struggle with the priests of his day in an attempt to loosen the binding of Judaic law and

Left: The Sermon on the Mount. *This painting by Cosimo Rosselli, shows Jesus speaking to his followers and curing a leper.*

allow uncircumcised Gentiles, women, and other "unclean" persons to participate more fully in the religious life of the Jews.

The "virgin birth," according to Thiering, can be explained by examining the disciplines to which Jesus' father Joseph, heir to the kingdom of David, was subject regarding marriage. Under the rules of the Essene sect to which Joseph belonged, a lengthy acquaintance with Mary culminated in a ceremony that amounted to a sort of public announcement of the couple's engagement. Sex—which was considered by the Essenes to be an activity of a lower order, but necessary to perpetuate the race— was to take place only three months later, when a marriage ceremony was performed for the first time. Once Mary had become pregnant, and had carried the child for three months, then a second marriage would take place. Apart from these ritual meetings, and occasional family reunions, the men and women of the sect would live apart, each fulfilling what was considered to be their primary commitment to religious life.

In the case of Joseph and Mary, Thiering concludes, the pregnancy happened immediately after the first of the three ceremonies, rather than after the first marriage as prescribed by the disciplines of their sect. In other words, they "jumped the gun," and Mary got pregnant during the time when she ought to have been still a virgin. Thiering even goes so far as to suggest that this cloud surrounding the circumstances of his birth was such a significant psychological factor in Jesus' life that it drove him more often than was prudent to take the side of the underdog in the political struggles of his day.

Thiering's political/historical approach to the life of Jesus classifies all the miracles of his life as neither factual nor mythological, but as elaborately coded records that can be read on two levels. One level, on the surface, is intended to be a simple teaching for the laity, who can benefit from the stories and parables contained in the scriptures. The other level, beneath the surface, is intended for the initiates and represents a detailed and accurate historical record, with the major players and their views preserved for posterity. At this level, Jesus turning water into wine at the Cana wedding feast becomes a rebellious and political act, granting not just baptism (water) but full initiation (wine) to those not previously considered worthy of it. "Heaven" becomes a physical place, an Essene sanctuary where initiation rites are performed, and "angels" become human priests and advisors. As for the resurrection, it never took place because Jesus never died. He survived a power play by Judas Iscariot, in which Pilate was simply used as a pawn, and lived to a ripe old age while continuing to direct his followers from behind the scenes.

Other speculations have Jesus traveling to India in his youth, where he learned his miracle arts from adepts of yoga, and to where he returned after he was saved from death on the cross. The twentieth-

Above: *In this fresco in the Aphendiko church, Christ is seen performing the miracle of turning water into wine, at the wedding in Cana.*

century mystic Gurdjieff, on the other hand, insists that Jesus never existed but was just an invention of those who could not find comfort in the idea of a remote, abstract, and seemingly whimsical God. His only connection with India was the similarity between the name "Christ" and the name "Krishna."

Whatever the truth might have been, the fact remains that Jesus, historical or mythological, is the figure around whom one of the world's major religions is built—a religion that has for centuries defined the parameters of the miraculous for most of the Western world. We now know that many of the wonders performed by Jesus have been performed by others, both among his own followers and among the shamans, healers, and adepts of other cultures and religions. This knowledge has presented a challenge to humankind to break through the territorial boundaries of its religious doctrines that would have been impossible in times before the advent of the "global village" of contemporary times.

It could even be said that the growing interest in

Jesus said:
He who is near me is near the fire,
and he who is far from me
is far from the kingdom.
His disciples said to him:
On what day does the kingdom come?
Jesus said:
It does not come when it is expected.
They will not say, Lo, here! or Lo, there!
But the kingdom of the Father
is spread out upon the earth, and men do
not see it.

-THE SECRET SAYINGS OF JESUS
ACCORDING TO THE GOSPEL OF THOMAS

discovering and synthesizing the common elements among the world's religions has replaced science as the primary threat to sectarian religious dogma. Science has proved, in the twentieth century, that it is not in and of itself the panacea for all human problems. It has become clear that unless spiritual or religious values are brought to bear on the uses of scientific technology, it can be immensely destructive to human life and the environment. In religious life we are faced with a choice, then, of whether to continue to battle for control of the territory of the human spirit or to allow the boundaries created by sectarianism to dissolve in the hope of discovering a higher, more unifying principle—a principle which might include not only Jesus but also Mohammed, Buddha, Lao Tzu, and many others.

This does not mean that the Judeo-Christian tradition would have nothing special to contribute. At its best, it is arguably more life-affirmative, more egalitarian, and puts more emphasis on love and service to one's fellow humans than many other religions. It doesn't even mean that Christians would have to give up

Above: This detail of a painting on silk shows a Taoist adept playing a flute in a Taoist paradise. Most religions have common elements, and Taoism recognizes a unifying principle, which though expressed differently within Christianity, has at its source a deep reverence for life.

their belief in the historical reality of the virgin birth and resurrection. But it does mean that they would have to allow that this was just one way in which the God chose to "signal" humanity of his continuing interest in their affairs; and that when Jesus insisted that "no man cometh unto the Father, but by me" he was speaking not to every race and nation on the planet but to a particular people at a particular time, under a particular set of circumstances.

If the traditional boundaries imposed by religious sectarianism were broken, the miraculous would be free to expand in all directions. Jesus, along with other mystics, shamans, miracle-workers, or yogis, would be just one of many such persons whose lives have brought the possibility of the impossible to humanity. The miraculous would belong not just to the Christian God and the Son who is his earthly representative, but to all human beings who invite it into their lives, in all places and times. It is with this possibility in mind that we enter this section on the life of Christianity's greatest miracle-worker, to explore some alternative conceptions of "what manner of man" Jesus was.

Jesus set the standard for miraculous transformations of food and drink by turning water into wine at a wedding, and multiplying loaves of bread at an outdoor picnic, and many of his more pious followers are reputed to have performed similar miracles. St. Bruno, for example, arrived at a Carthusian monastery to find the monks seated stunned and motionless before plates full of fowl which had by some mistake been prepared for them even though it was Friday. Bruno calmly sat down at the table, made the sign of the cross over the forbidden birds, and changed them into tortoises so they could be eaten. St. Ulrich of Augsburg is so famous for transforming a joint of meat on a similar occasion that images of him often feature a fish. Teresa of Avila reportedly increased a month's supply of flour to a quantity more than ample to meet the needs of her convent for half a year with God's help. St. Sorus, after curing the sixth-century King of Burgundy of leprosy, celebrated the occasion with a feast and three barrels of wine miraculously squeezed from just three grapes picked from a nearby vineyard. But one of the most charming of these tales of food conversion is told about St. Nicolas of Tolentino, and combines transformation of food with an extraordinary raising of the dead. It is said that when Nicholas lay dying, he was so thin and wasted that his grieving companions undertook to prepare a delicately dressed dish of doves for him to eat, hoping to tempt him into taking some food. But Nicolas had never eaten animal food in his life, and he certainly wasn't going to start now. The story, told in Montague Summers' *The Physical Phenomena of Mysticism*, goes on to say:

Painfully raising himself on his poor pallet, Nicolas stretched his hands over the dish, and lo! the birds rejoicing were in a flash covered with plumage, and

Above: *A portrait of St. Nicolas of Tolentino, who performed many miracles, even one on his deathbed.*

flew out of the window of his little whitewashed cell towards the blue sky beyond. But they hovered around until in a few days the Saint breathed his last, when they were seen mounting into the air, accompanying (as it is piously believed) his soul to Paradise. For as he breathed his last the room was filled with a heavenly fragrance, as of lilies, and gleamed with a radiant light.

Right: *This beautiful painting* The Marriage Feast at Cana *by Gerard David* (1460-1523) *shows Jesus performing the miracle of turning water into wine.*

The miracle
of Walking on Water

The disciple Peter failed to walk on the water because of his doubt. But subsequent Peters are reported to have succeeded in the task--Peter of Alcántara, a Franciscan, Peter of Nolasco of the Mercedarians, and the Dominican Peter Gonzales. Our continuing fascination with this powerful symbol of the miraculous abilities of Jesus is reflected in its appearance in contemporary movies and cartoons. Actor Peter Sellers joins the list of Peters able to perform this extraordinary feat in the movie *Being There*, featuring a character who is too simple and innocent to cope with the stresses of modern-day life.

Jesus as Miracle-Worker

And in the fourth watch of the night Jesus went unto them, walking on the sea.

And when the disciples saw him walking on the sea, they were troubled, saying, It is a spirit; and they cried out for fear.

But straightway Jesus spake unto them, saying, Be of good cheer; it is I; be not afraid.

And Peter answered him and said, Lord, if it be thou, bid me come unto thee on the water.

And he said, Come. And when Peter was come down out of the ship, he walked on the water, to go to Jesus.

But when he saw the wind boisterous, he was afraid; and beginning to sink, he cried, saying, Lord, save me.

And immediately Jesus stretched forth his hand, and caught him, and said unto him, O thou of little faith, wherefore didst thou doubt?

[MATTHEW 14:25-31]

The act Matthew describes of Jesus walking on the water is one of the most captivating miracles of the New Testament. Its sheer magic seems to touch the child in each of us, and Peter echoes our childlike wonder in his response to the magic before him. He wants to try it, too, just like every child wants to duplicate a marvelous act that he sees for the first time. And, with the same kind of faith that every child has that he or she can do some marvelous thing, Peter steps out onto the water and ...

Suddenly realizes it's not as simple as it looks!

Or is that not perhaps the whole point of this story? That in fact it is as simple as it looks, and it is our belief that it is somehow difficult—our doubt— which brings in the fear and trembling that prevents us from doing "impossible" things.

Interestingly enough, it is in this "foretaste of a Nature that is in the future" that we find the most

evidence that it is quite possible that Jesus really did "walk on the water," at least through some method of levitation. The Yoga Sutras of Patanjali, legendary Indian sage who is believed to have lived some two thousand years before Christ, allude to the possibility as follows:

By directing the power of the breath towards the relationship between the body and the space around it, the body becomes as light as floating cobwebs, and through meditation on these he travels through space.

This explanation would fit with the theories that Jesus spent several years in India during the time of his life that is not recorded in the Gospels, where he might have learned the techniques of yoga. But it is equally possible that the powers of levitation came to Jesus spontaneously, as an outcome of his enlightened state. Patanjali was, in addition to being a mystic, a scientist who observed phenomena and then sought to explain and systematize them. He didn't invent the phenomena himself—he had seen

Left: *This mosaic by Giotto and Cavallini, which adorns the atrium of St. Peter's Basilica in Rome, shows Jesus stilling the tempest and walking on water.*

people who, through the practice of yoga, found that they were able to levitate.

Many shamanistic traditions also speak of levitation as one of the powers of healers and "clever men", and the records of the Catholic Church are full of reports of saintly flights, many of them attested to by sober and reliable witnesses. In fact the ability to levitate has been so common among contemplative mystics that it is not considered by the Church to be of itself a proof of saintliness. When the aerial displays take place in public, it can even be a cause for consternation to Church authorities, as it often was in the case of Joseph of Copertino (1603-1663).

Joseph was a carpenter's son, by all accounts a simple and innocent but often irascible fellow, who could be transported into ecstasy—and above the heads of his fellow monks at prayer—at the drop of a hat. Interested in religious life quite early, he was experiencing religious ecstasies by the time he was eight years old. He was quickly expelled from the Capucin lay order of the priesthood he entered soon after his sixteenth birthday because of his absentminded and erratic behavior, and wandered about for several months until he

persuaded another monastic order to take him in. There he practiced such austeries as wearing a hair shirt and flagellating himself. He eventually joined an order of St. Francis in Altamura, where he became a priest at the age of twenty-five. But Joseph was obviously still a bit troublesome to his superiors, because he was appearing before a Church council to answer charges of heresy when, during Mass at the monastery where he was staying as a guest, he was observed by several nuns to soar through the air from one corner of the sanctuary towards the altar, where he alighted briefly before being swept back into the air again and returned to his place. He must have been cleared of the heresy charges, because the next record of his extraordinary abilities comes from Rome, where he was observed to rise off the ground as he knelt to kiss the feet of Pope Urban III. Still later, in Assisi, he apparently soared about fifteen feet above the heads of an assembled group of worshippers in order to kiss a portrait of the Virgin Mary.

"In the Church of Santa Chiara in Copertino," reports anthropologist Eric Dingwall in his book, *Some Human Oddities* (1947), "a festival was once in progress in honor of the clothing of some novitiates. Joseph was present, and was on his knees in a

---

Above: Joseph of Copertino, a carpenter's son, was known for his ability to levitate.
He was often a source of embarrassment to Church authorities because he sometimes soared through the air at
inopportune moments, frequently in front of many witnesses.

The miracles of Alfonso Liguori

The miracles of Alfonso Liguori, founder of the Redemptorist Order, were unusually well authenticated as the proceedings for beatification began almost immediately after his death. Three canons and members of the congregation testified that when he was in Amalfi in 1750, he had levitated while preaching a sermon; and fellow members of his Order described how they had seen him floating when he was rapt in prayer in his cell. Even when, towards his death, he became a cripple in a wheel chair he still occasionally shot up into the air, on one occasion knocking his head against the chin of Fr. Volpicelli, who happened to be bending over him at the time. At their next meeting, a witness noticed that Volpicelli was careful to keep at a safe distance; wisely, as the levitation was repeated. Liguori's most celebrated miracle took place in 1774 when, preparing to celebrate mass, he went into a trance and on coming out of it two hours later, said he had been at Pope Clement XIV's deathbed in Rome. This caused some amusement to those present. We were all tempted to burst out laughing, Sister Agatha Viscardi was to recall. But then those who were in attendance at the bedside of the dying Pope Clement described how they had not only seen, but talked to Alfonso; he had led them in prayers for the dying.

corner of the church, when the words *Veni Sponsa Cristi* (Come, Bride of Christ) were being intoned. Giving his accustomed cry, he ran towards the convent's father confessor, a priest from Secli, a village not far off, and who was attending the service and, seizing him, grasped him by the hand and . . . finally both rose into the air . . . the one borne aloft by Joseph and the other by God Himself, both being sons of St. Francis, the one being beside himself with fear but the other with sanctity."

But perhaps the most often-quoted levitation stories about the colorful Joseph was that which occurred while he was walking in the garden with the Reverend Antonio Chiarello. Chiarello remarked how beautiful was "the heaven that God had made" and Joseph immediately gave a cry and soared to the top of a nearby olive tree, where he spent the better part of an hour perched delicately on a branch. When he finally came back to himself he had to be rescued with a ladder.

Teresa of Avila, the sixteenth-century saint—whose autobiographical writings have a quality that would persuade even the most cynical that she was utterly sincere and truthful—describes events where she was "levitated" quite against her own wishes:

This has happened only rarely. Once, however, it took place when we were all together in the choir, and I was on my knees, about to take Communion. This distressed me very much, for it seemed a most extraordinary thing and likely to arouse considerable talk.

Teresa was not so much impressed by what was happening to her as she was embarrassed, and particularly once when it happened during a sermon where "some great ladies were present." Even though she tried to resist the levitation by lying on the floor and getting some of the sisters to hold her down, she was nevertheless observed. After this event, Teresa says, she "earnestly beseeched the Lord to grant me no more favors if they must have outward and visible signs." She was pleased to report that God seemed to have granted her prayerful wishes, because it was otherwise impossible for her to prevent these extraordinary happenings:

"You feel and see yourself carried away you know not whither," she said of the experience. "For though we feel how delicious it is, yet the weakness of our nature makes us afraid at first...so trying is it that I would very often resist and exert all my strength, particularly at those times when the rapture was

---

Right: *Another picture of St. Joseph of Copertino, shown here during one of his levitations.*

coming on me in public. I did so, too, very often when I was alone, because I was afraid of delusions. Occasionally I was able, by great efforts, to make a slight resistance, but afterwards I was worn out, like a person who had been contending with a strong giant; at other times it was impossible to resist at all; my soul was carried away, and almost always my head with it—I had no power over it—and now and then the whole body as well, so that it was lifted up from the ground."

Right: *St. Theresa of Avila, a mystical saint of the sixteenth century, was also known to levitate quite against her own wishes.*

Jesus as Healer

And when Jesus was come into Peter's house, he saw his wife's mother laid, and sick of a fever.

And he touched her hand, and the fever left her: and she arose, and ministered unto them.

When the even was come, they brought unto him many that were possessed with devils: and he cast out the spirits with his word, and healed all that were sick.

[MATTHEW 8:14-16]

Religion, it has been said, exists to heal our disease. In the more recent history of humankind, the healing of physical diseases has been more and more relegated to science, while religion considers the

Right: *Christ healing the mother of Simon Peter, by J. Bridges,* (1818-1854).

The miracle of Saint Catherine

There are many records of saints' bodies being dug up years after burial, and being found incorrupt. This phenomenon is not confined to Catholic holy men or women, but there are more on record because of the custom of exhuming saints. A good example of the phenomenon is St Catherine Labouré, who died in 1876 in Paris (France). Her body was buried in a triple coffin in a chapel crypt in the city and lay undisturbed for fifty-six years until it was exhumed on 21 March 1933 in preparation for her beatification. A surgeon who witnessed the exhumation reported:

The body was carefully taken out of the coffin and placed on a long table.
In examining the body we noticed the perfect suppleness of the arms and legs. These members have merely undergone a slight mummification. The skin throughout was intact and like parchment. The muscles were preserved; we could easily dissect them in a study of anatomy.

We cut the sternum on the median line. The bone showed a cartilaginous, elastic consistency and was easily cut by the surgeonís knife. The thoracid cavity being opened it was easy for us to remove the heart. It was much shrunken but it had kept its shape. We could easily see within it the little fibrous cords, remains of the valves and muscles. We also took out a number of the ribs and clavicle. We disjointed the arms—these two will be conserved apart. The two knee caps were taken out. The fingers and toe nails were in perfect condition. The hair remained attached to the scalp.
The eyes were in the orbits; the eyelids half closed; we were able to state that the ball though fallen and shrunken existed in its entirety, and even the color, bluish grey, of the iris still remained. The ears were intact......

"dis-ease" of the spirit to be its proper domain. But it has always been apparent that the two forms are not so easily separated. The word "health" is linguistically connected to the word "whole," and the wholeness of human beings demands that we take into account the essential interdependence of the body, the mind, and the spirit.

The earliest nomadic cultures had no use for written scripture or churches. But they did have a need for healing from time to time, of their physical, psychological, and spiritual discomforts. And this function of healing was performed by men and women very much like Jesus—able to drive out both physical and psychological demons from the afflicted in ways that seem quite magical and miraculous to us today. There are some important differences, of course, and it would be an oversimplification to insist that Jesus was really a shaman. He was not, as far as we know, trained in the herbal remedies and other forms of medicine known to most tribal cultures. He also did not appear to regard himself as primarily a healer, although the New Testament Gospel narratives suggest that it was his healing miracles that first brought so many people to hear him.

But Jesus had bigger fish to fry, and in the larger story of his life, the healing miracles form only a footnote. The central issue to him, it seems, was faith. And this faith, if one could cultivate it properly, could not only heal physical and psychological diseases, it could heal the "disease" of humanness itself. Faith could reunite a person with the Kingdom of God, whether that kingdom was perceived to be within, in the here and now, or without, in the hereafter. The goal, in that sense, was not so different from the goal of the tribal shamans. But the culture in which Jesus lived was quite different from the tribal cultures, and so required a different approach to the remedy of disease. The people of Judea were arguably less "whole" than their tribal ancestors, already long separated from a Kingdom of God which was apparent in every feature of the landscape. In inviting his contemporaries to have faith in him, Jesus was inviting them to share in his own wholeness, and thereby reclaim that lost Kingdom which he had found.

Whatever the subtleties of the real message of Jesus, the healing miracles have been perceived as an ongoing proof of his holiness and the holiness of the many Christian saints who followed him. From the earliest days of the Apostles to the televised extravaganzas of modern-day evangelical preachers, it has been clear that "faith heals." Faith heals in the waters of Lourdes, in the laying-on-of-hands, and in prayers to the saints. The blind see, the lame walk, and the deaf regain their hearing. Demons are exorcised and broken lives become whole. The fact that some charlatans have exploited the suffering of others, and betrayed their faith through deceit and fraud, is doubly unfortunate. Not only are the immediate victims of fraud disappointed, and in

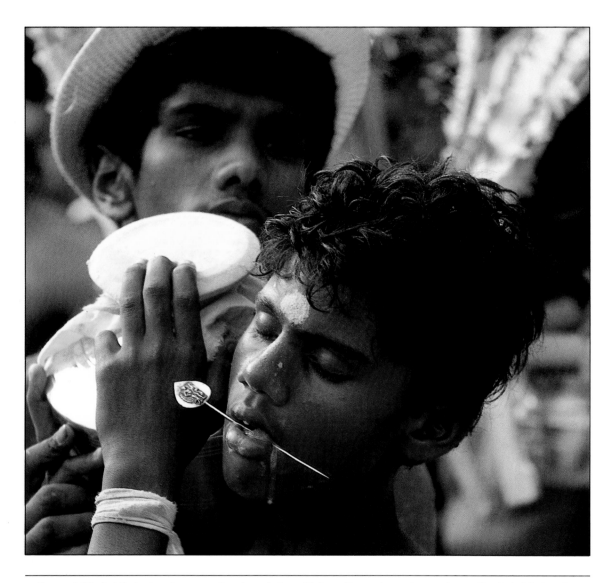

Above: A Hindu pilgrim in a trance undergoing what would, in ordinary circumstances, be a rather painful operation. This shows the power of the mind to overcome physical pain, or in some cases, physical ailments.

some cases even endangered, but the whole phenomenon has tended to be tarnished with guilt by association.

One of the real dilemmas presented by "faith healing" lies in the fact that the mind does indeed, under the right circumstances, have an extraordinary power over the body. The use of hypnosis in place of anesthesia to block sensations of pain in surgery is just one outstanding example of this fact. But pain is also one of the primary tools the body uses in communicating its distress. The danger is that healers, with the best intentions in the world, can interfere with the functioning of this important tool to the extent that the patient feels "cured" while in fact his or her disease is now free to work its damage without sending any signals that something is wrong. For this reason, the most reputable healers will always insist that a patient be examined using more orthodox medical diagnostic procedures. In this way they can be certain that their own healing techniques are being used to assist in real recovery rather than just to mask the symptoms of a serious illness.

Most doctors now admit the possibility that up to eighty percent of human disease has a significant psychological component. In other words, the way we think with our minds, and feel with our emotions, has a profound effect on the health of our bodies. It is common sense, really, but a common sense that has long been overlooked in orthodox medical science. If it is true, then many miraculous healings also "make sense"—where the mental,

CRITERIA FOR CERTIFYING MIRACULOUS HEALINGS

1.
The disability or malady should be serious.

2.
The patient should not have already been improving at the time of the healing, nor suffering from a condition that normally might be expected to improve.

3.
The patient should not have been under orthodox medical treatment at the time.

4.
The healing should be sudden and instantaneous.

5.
The cure must be perfect and complete.

6.
The cure should not occur at a time when a crisis due to natural causes has affected the patient or the illness.

7.
The cure must be permanent.

Above: *Pierre de Rudder was a Belgian man who had his leg broken by a falling tree in 1867. He refused amputation and suffered constant pain. In April 1875, he made a pilgrimage to the shrine of Our Lady of Lourdes in Oostakker, Belgium, where he received a miracle cure. He walked normally until his death in 1898.*

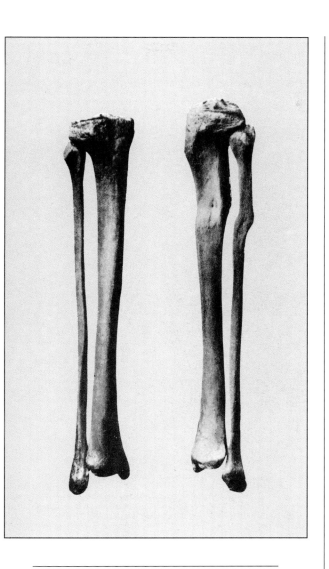

Above *This photograph shows his right and left legs after his death, showing the growth of bone at the fracture point.*

emotional or spiritual crisis that has contributed to a disease is healed by the experience of wholeness and connection with the divine that we call "faith," the body is suddenly freed to start repairing itself—as it is admirably equipped to do under the right circumstances. In recognition of this complex interdependence between body, mind and spirit, the Catholic Church has tried to distinguish truly "miraculous" healings from those which can be explained by the dynamics of psychosomatic disease.

The study of one of the more famous and well documented recent miraculous healings at Lourdes is told in the book, *The Extraordinary Cure of Vittorio Michelli.* In 1962, Michelli was suffering from a large, cancerous tumor on his left hip which had resulted in such severe disintegration of his hip bone that the bone of his upper leg was left floating in a mass of tissue. Desperate, he traveled to Lourdes, where he says that during his first bath in the waters he felt a sensation of heat moving through his body. Feeling much better, he took several more baths before returning home, where he continued to improve and finally went back to his doctors, insisting that they X-ray his hip to see if any improvement had taken place. In fact, they discovered that the tumor had become smaller—a fact so interesting that they continued to document his recovery over the next several months. This spontaneous remission is not unheard-of in medical history, but the regeneration of the bone is considered to be impossible.

Faith and Betrayal of Faith in Healing

In a 1957 article in the Journal of Prospective Techniques, entitled "Psychological Variables in Human Cancer," psychologist Bruno Klopfer describes a sequence of events surrounding one of his patients who was suffering from cancer of the lymph nodes.

This form of cancer is particularly voracious, and the patient was in the advanced stages of the disease. His body was riddled with tumors, and it seemed he could survive only a few weeks at most. But he was also a man determined to live, and he had just heard of a new drug called Krebiozen that had shown great promise in treating lymphatic cancer. He managed to persuade his doctor to give him an injection of the new wonder drug, despite the fact that it was recommended only for patients whose cancer was not so far advanced.

Just three days after the injection the man was out of bed for the first time in weeks, and walking around. Tests showed that his tumors were half their original size. By the time another week had passed the tumors were completely gone, and he was able to leave the hospital and resume most of his normal activities. He remained healthy for about two months, and then articles began to appear suggesting that Krebiozen actually had no significant effect on cancer of the lymph nodes. Soon after reading these reports the patient suffered a relapse and was re-admitted to the hospital. His doctor, knowing that nothing could be done, nevertheless decided to try an experiment. He told the patient that a new version of Krebiozen had just been produced that was proving to be much more effective than the first. He then injected the patient with a placebo, and once again the improvement was dramatic. The tumors melted away and he was able to leave the hospital again.

Finally, though, the American Medical Association announced that a nationwide study of Krebiozen had shown that the drug was totally ineffective in treating cancer. This last breach of the patient's "faith" turned out to be fatal. The cancer reappeared as suddenly as it had gone, and he was dead within a matter of days.

The miracle of Maria Van Laer

There was an interesting case involving Maria Van Laer, who was born early in the twentieth century in northern Belgium. When she was sixteen, she contracted osteomyelitis, along with a number of associated afflictions. A devout Catholic, she went five times on pilgrimages to Lourdes, but although this alleviated her suffering slightly, there was no cure. Her doctor gave up on her.

Then in 1933, at Beauraing, in her own country and practically on her own doorstep, some children had a vision of the Virgin Mary, which had the usual result of inspiring people to make pilgrimages to the site of the alleged encounters. Maria, who to all appearances was close to death, implored her family to take her there. Her aunt and two nursing sisters had her driven to the site.

Next morning, when Maria was back home, the affliction that had crippled her for sixteen years was gone. The doctors who examined her pronounced her cure inexplicable. She subsequently became a nun. Her cure was officially recognized by the Church as a miracle, and for nearly half a century after being considered at death's door, she lived, dying as Sister Prudentia in 1980.

Above: *This detail from Jesus walking on water captures the fear in Peter's face, as doubt surfaces as to his ability to join his master on the water.*

Jesus as Mystic

And there arose a great storm of wind, and the waves beat into the ship, so that it was now full. And he was in the hinder part of the ship, asleep on a pillow: and they awake him, and say unto him, Master, carest thou not that we perish?

And he arose, and rebuked the wind, and said unto the sea, Peace, be still. And the wind ceased, and there was a great calm.

And he said unto them, Why are ye so fearful? how is it that ye have no faith?

And they feared exceedingly, and said one to another, What manner of man is this, that even the wind and the sea obey him?

(MARK 4.37-41)

According to the religions of the East, such as Hinduism, Taoism and Buddhism, to undertake the religious life is to set out on a path from samsara to nirvana, from disharmony to harmony, from sleep to awakening. This transformation has happened to many individuals throughout the ages, and depends not on the details of behavior but on the level of the individual's own inner understanding. It is, in essence, a shift from identification with the separate, individual ego, towards union with the divine. Put in terms more familiar to Christians, the mystic view holds that not only Jesus but everyone is potentially a "Son of God." Not all those who have realized their potential have the ability and desire to communicate their experience. But those who do—who are "chosen" or "called" to the task—are called Masters, and try to teach others through example, allegory, and parable, how to undertake their own spiritual journey towards the same enlightened state. The only "judgment day" is that moment in every seeker's life when he or she is finally confronts the choice between continued identification with the transient

joys and sufferings of earthly life, and "rebirth" into a life of identification with the eternal.

Since the discovery in the mid-1940s of the *Nag Hammadi* texts, including what claim to be the "secret teachings of the living Jesus," this view of Jesus as mystic has been given new life among Western biblical scholars. The texts reflect the views long thought to be held by the Gnostic Christians, associated with Thomas in India. The Gnostics appear to have been quite influential in the first century following the crucifixion, but were declared to be heretics by the end of the second century A.D. Their fondness for quoting the Fourth Gospel of John even threatened that remarkable book's inclusion in the Christian canon for a time. But it is not strictly necessary to use either John's Gospel or the *Nag Hammadi* texts in order to view Jesus as a mystic comparable to, say, Buddha, or Zen Masters like Rinzai. Viewed through Eastern lenses, even such well-known "nature miracles" as Jesus calming the storm on the Sea of Galilee can be seen as "secret teachings" with a distinctly mystical flavor—even though one might have to jump a few hurdles at first in order to see them as such.

Left: *St. Thomas' tomb in India is a site of pilgrimage for many people.*

It is also a bit of an "exercise"—some of the Gospels lend themselves more easily to such interpretations than others and, quite frankly, if one is interested in Jesus-as-mystic it is more rewarding to look into the "Secret Gospel of Thomas" than into the pages of the New Testament. But it is an instructive exercise, nevertheless; before taking leave of the extraordinary miracle-worker called Jesus it can remind us how very many different costumes have been placed upon him since his humble birth amidst the animals in a stable in Bethlehem.

The act of Christ "stilling the tempest" is relatively minor league, as New Testament miracles go, and so an easy target for the skeptical. Mere coincidence, says the confirmed unbeliever. Those who give Jesus more credit might say that he was, perhaps, one of those men very sensitive to the nuances of weather and could therefore sleep happily through a brief squall, knowing it would pass soon. It was just convenient timing—his disciples undoubtedly waited until they were at their wits' end before disturbing their Master's rest. And, just as the impatient diner finally gives in to the urge to light a cigarette and thereby brings the waiter with the food, so does the amount of time for disciples to reach their wits' end correspond to the length of a squall on the sea of Galilee.

One of the more interesting features of this story, though, is the distinct nuances given to it by the different Gospels. We must assume that, in common with the writers of all scriptures, the authors of the Gospels chose their words with as much care as they were capable of, and that their words can reveal much about the assumptions underlying them. In approaching the miracle of stilling the tempest with the aim in mind of extracting its mystical significance, we find a marked contrast between Mark's version of the story quoted above, and the version told by Matthew, widely believed to have been written later than Mark, and to have used Mark as its primary source. Matthew's version is as follows:

And when he was entered into a ship, his disciples followed him.

And behold, there arose a great tempest in the sea, insomuch that the ship was covered with the waves: but he was asleep.

And his disciples came to him, and awoke him, saying, Lord, save us: we perish.

And he saith unto them, Why are ye fearful, O ye of little faith? When he arose, and rebuked the winds and the sea, and there was a great calm.

But the men marveled, saying, What manner of man is this, that even the winds and the sea obey him!

In Matthew's account, Jesus chastises his disciples immediately, when they first wake him up. It is only after this that he goes out to calm the storm. They wake him with the words, "Lord, save us: we perish"—quite a different frame of mind than the one that asks, "carest thou not that we perish?"

Above: *A detail of the disciples' boat in the storm.*

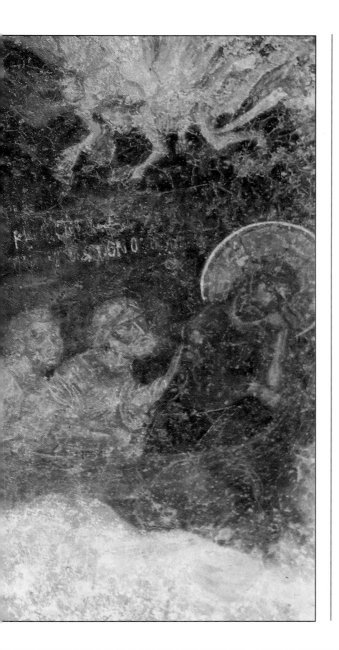

Mark's tale is altogether more amenable to the mystical, or Eastern approach. The disciples use the word "Master," which has long been used in the East but is so rare in the Western spiritual literature that most of us have come to associate it entirely with its secular meaning of control and domination, or, rather more archaically, of excellence in craftsmanship. Jesus' handling of the situation here is also quite different from the thunderous, patriarchal mood conveyed by Matthew. As Mark tells it, the response of Jesus to his disciples' alarm is to quietly get up and direct Mother Nature to settle down. It is only after the storm has abated that he delivers his message about faith and fear. Matthew's Jesus, on the other hand, gives his fearful disciples a scolding as soon as they wake him up, thereby quite likely adding guilt to their already panicky state.

In asking, "carest thou not that we perish?" the disciples in Mark's account also reflect a more "Eastern" frame of mind. First, their question assumes that Jesus has been aware of the storm even as he was asleep. It is understood as one of the characteristics of enlightened Masters in the East that their awareness is constant, even when they are

Left: *Jesus walking on water and stilling the wind—taken from a mural painted in the thirteenth century, in Hagia Sophia, Trabzon, Turkey.*

Above: *Just as the storm on the sea of Gallilee arose and subsided, so too we can experience sudden storms today.*

calmly sleeping when our ship is being swamped by the waves?

As allegory viewed through Eastern lenses, then, the stilling of the tempest in Mark's version becomes the story of a man who lives always at the center of the cyclone, and who uses this situation of the storm to teach his disciples an important lesson about inner stillness in the midst of outer storms. The lesson for the disciples is that if they can find this stillness in themselves they need not fear even death. In calming the storm Jesus shows that this stillness is contagious, and even the wildest of storms will respond and fall in tune. His chastisement of the disciples at the end is gentle, questioning: "Why are ye so fearful? how is it that ye have no faith?" He invites them to examine how their fear prevents them from being available to this contagion of stillness—a fear that Nature herself clearly does not suffer from.

Matthew's Jesus by contrast is a bit macho, playing more the role of the Son of an angry Jehovah. His disciples, correspondingly, exhibit considerably more fear of the storm—"Save us!" The result is that the mystical allegory of the center of the cyclone is more difficult to extract. It becomes, in the end, more akin to some kind of power trip than something wondrous and divine. And, as such, it resists being pulled out of the pages of miracle history and installed in the annals of timeless truth it is méant to convey.

physically sleeping. Second, the question is not necessarily first and foremost about survival, nor does it demand that their Master "save" them. It can be taken as a question about attitude, about consciousness: Does it matter to you that we are all about to die? How can you be lying down here

The Symbolism of the Miraculous

One of the contemporary classics of commentary on the Fourth Gospel of John was written by Cambridge scholar C. H. Dodd, titled The Interpretation of the Fourth Gospel *and first published in 1953.*

The work is not particularly suited for mass consumption, filled as it is with scholarly references to previous commentaries and liberally laced with untranslated Greek and Hebrew. But even a superficial dip into its pages affords an eye-opening glimpse into that sector of biblical scholarship which considers the symbolic meaning of the life and teachings of Jesus.

The Fourth Gospel records only eight of the many miracles attributed to Jesus in the other Gospel narratives. It has been pointed out that in John, there is a precise literary structure of correspondences between the miracles, and of their place in revealing the overall purpose of Jesus' life in the divine plan. These are details which we will not go into here, despite their elegance and appeal, because it would take us far into a thicket of theological discourse from which we might never extract ourselves. Instead, we'll take the briefest of samplings from the banquet on offer, so that those who are interested in the symbolism of the miraculous might be steered in the direction of further inquiry.

The first of these eight "signs" takes place during the wedding at Cana, where Jesus turns water into wine. According to Dodd, who supports his argument with a careful explanation of the social and historical context in which the book was written, the "water" in this case symbolizes "the entire system of Jewish ceremonial observance—and by implication for religion upon that level, wherever it is found." This view is consistent with the view of Barbara Thiering discussed earlier, as is the corresponding interpretation of the wine as symbolic of the new, living religiousness that Jesus brings to replace what has become mere empty ritual. Dodd also quotes the early Church Father Origen, who said "And truly before Jesus the Scripture was water, but from the time of Jesus it has become wine to us."

The second and third signs are related both by virtue of being healing miracles and, says Dodd, in being demonstrations of the power of the "Word"—the Word in this sense meaning the truth of one who knows, as opposed to the sayings of one who is well versed in the scriptures. The first of the two healings happens in response to the plea of a nobleman who approaches Jesus on behalf of his son. The boy is dying, at a place some distance away, so Jesus does not heal him by touching him but merely by declaring him to be healed. He rescues him from the immediate threat of death and destruction. The boy's father, furthermore, must accept what Jesus says, must trust him without any immediate factual proof, as he walks back home and discovers that indeed the boy has been healed.

In the second of the two healing miracles, Jesus is confronted with a very different sort of illness. The man next to the well—symbolic again of the existing ceremonies and rituals of religion—has been crippled for thirty-eight years without being made whole. But this incident is not seen just as an indictment of the old traditions, but also of those who have declined to use even the healing waters that are available to them. Have you the will to

Left: *Bread remains a powerful symbol of life even today, as depicted by Pontormo in his painting* Cena in Emmaus.

Above: *When the exiles were starving in the desert, Moses prayed to God who brought forth water and manna to feed them. Painted in the fifteenth century by an unknown artist.*

become a healthy man? asks Jesus. The implication is that he has not, heretofore, and the answer the man offers in return is a rather feeble excuse. In this case, the power of the Word is given directly, and with dramatic results. The will to live is the issue here, and in response to the truth and authority of Jesus, the man takes up his bed and walks.

The fourth miracle, the Feeding of the Multitude, is connected with the Old Testament legend of the exiles under Moses being sustained by manna from God. But here too, the spiritual significance of the story is extracted only by putting aside the material, phenomenal aspects of the miracle and looking into what it says about the revolutionary message Jesus was trying to convey. When the multitude was fed in this miraculous way, many of them wanted to make Jesus a King then and there. He retreated to a mountaintop to avoid them, and the miracle of walking on the water follows. Dodd passes lightly over the significance of this miracle in a footnote, suggesting that perhaps it was meant "to suggest the symbolism of divine power and majesty employed in...passages of the Old Testament." Overall, he suggests that the incident refers to a period of doubt

and potential separation on the part of the disciples which is almost immediately put to rest by Jesus' appearance to them in this way.

After this interlude Jesus confronts those who want to declare him King because of the miraculous feeding, saying in essence that they have misunderstood the "sign." What he brings is not physical nourishment for the body, but spiritual nourishment for the soul: "Moses gave you not that bread from heaven; but my Father giveth you the true bread from heaven. For the bread of God is he which cometh down from heaven, and giveth life unto the world." In the dialogue which follows the assembly seems to have taken him quite literally, to the point that even his disciples seem to think he is suggesting they cannibalize his own body. But the deeper significance probably lies in the fact that in essence, Jesus was hinting that he was in a sense God. Theologically speaking this was a scandalous assertion, and it is in this atmosphere of outrage and the debates that followed it that the scene is set for the next miracle, the "triumph of light over darkness" as Jesus heals the beggar who was born blind.

Right: *The triumph of light over darkness when Christ healed a blind man at the pool of Siloam. Taken from a fifteenth century mural in the monastery of St John Lampadistis, Cyprus.*

In pointing to the symbolism of the incident, Dodd refers us to the subsequent trial of the beggar, suggesting that it reflects the situation of all Christians who have been "enlightened in baptism and [are] called upon to confess Christ before men." The healed man, he says, "stands before his betters, to be badgered into denying the one thing of which he is certain . . . But the defendant proper is Jesus himself . . . [who] swiftly turns the tables on His judges, and pronounces sentence: 'For judgment I have come into the world, that the blind may see and the seeing may be blinded . . . If you were blind, no guilt would attach to you; but now you say, "We are the men who see: and you stand guilty."'"

In other words, Jesus brings the message that it is not ignorance of the truth that is a sin. The real guilt attaches to those who, believing that they know the truth because they have learned it from the scriptures, or have inherited it as a belief from their ancestors, judge others on the basis of their own unquestioned prejudices.

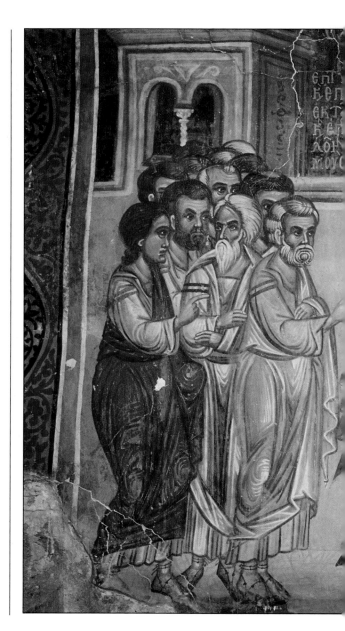

Part Four
Miracles Challenged:
The Search for Proof

According to conventional history, what we now know as the "Shroud of Turin" first surfaced in a French church in 1353. Geoffroy de Charny, Lord of Savoy, had built in that year a church at Lirey to honor the Blessed Virgin Mary, and endowed it with the wondrous relic in his possession, a long strip of linen cloth purported to be the burial shroud of the crucified Christ.

From there, the Shroud was eventually taken to Turin, where it has been ever since. In 1988 the Vatican allowed small samples of the shroud to be carbon dated, a scientific procedure that many had long desired to perform but which had been impossible before this time because the size of the samples required for the tests would have been too large. With improvements in carbon dating technology, it was possible to remove just a small, unobtrusive strip from one edge of the cloth. The results of these tests revealed that the linen was medieval, woven some time between 1260 and 1390.

The Shroud of Turin was declared, therefore, to be a medieval forgery.

Many people, however, remain unconvinced, for many reasons. Foremost among them is the image on the Shroud itself. It shows the body of a man, front and back, with bloodstains corresponding precisely with the tortures Jesus was described to have suffered on the day of the crucifixion. Furthermore, these stains are not consistent with medieval portrayals of the Passion, where Christ is most often nailed to the cross through the palms of his hands, and his head encircled by a wreath of thorns. Instead, the Shroud image reflects a more accurate picture of the actual practices in Jesus' time. The "crown of thorns" was in fact more like a cap that covered, and wounded, the whole skull. The wounds from the nails appear at the wrists, which was in fact where the nails were placed so that they would support the whole weight of a human body—a fact which has been confirmed in the Christian West only in the 1960s. The sheer level of detail in the image is persuasive in itself—it includes marks of

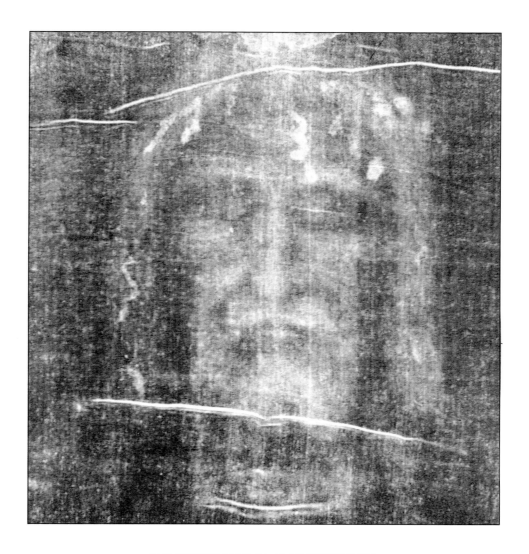

Above: *A detail from the Shroud of Turin.*

Above: *It is speculated that the Knights Templar were at one time entrusted to keep safe the Shroud of Turin, which is thought to be the basis of some of their practices. They were eventually charged with heresy and persecuted by the Inquisition, painted here by Goya.*

468

the flogging Jesus suffered, indicating that he had been hit as many as 125 times by a three-pronged whip commonly used by the Roman soldiers of the day.

Previous tests on the Shroud had revealed that the image was not painted, and analysis of the pigmentation compared favorably with the composition of dried blood. Pollen samples lifted off the fabric in other tests had matched plants growing in Palestine during Jesus' time. The fabric itself was of a weave used in Palestine, but not thought to be known in medieval Europe. Of course, the fabric could have been obtained during the crusades somehow and taken to Europe where the forgery was made. But if the Shroud were a work of art by a clever forger, all the other evidence suggested that the forgery itself would have had to have been something of a miracle. Countless efforts by skeptics to reproduce something similar to it had failed.

In their recent book, *The Jesus Conspiracy,* Holger Kersten and Elmar R. Gruber advance a thoroughly researched and persuasive argument that the Shroud of Turin is the real thing. They trace its history back to Edessa and a legend about the Mandylion, a mysterious linen portrait of Christ "not made by human hands." From there, the authors argue, the shroud was brought to Constantinople sometime in the tenth century, where it was kept in the Church of Our Lady Holy Mary of Blachernae. They quote a Frankish knight of the Fourth Crusade, Robert de

Above: *This beautiful depiction of the crucifixion of Jesus on the tree of the cross was painted in the fourteenth century by Italian artist Taddeo Gaddi.*

Clari, who writes in his August 1203 journals about "the shroud in which our Lord was wrapped, which was held up on display every Friday so that the figure of our Lord could be clearly seen." Kersten and Gruber by and large agree with other historians of the Shroud in speculating that the cloth was at some point given over to the keeping of the Knights Templar. They further argue that the image of the face on the Shroud was the basis of the mysterious "bearded head" the Templars were accused of worshipping in their secret rituals. And, as do other historians, they explore the possible relationship between the Frenchman Geoffroy de Charny and one Geoffroy de Charnay, a Templar who was burned at the stake along with Jacques de Molay at the time the Templars were charged with heresy and persecuted by the Inquisition.

But what about the carbon dating tests? Kersten and Gruber allege—backed up by painstaking research and analysis—that the tests were faked with the help of Vatican officials. The samples analyzed, they claim, were not from the Shroud at all but from a bit of medieval fabric. Correction: there was one sample taken from the Shroud itself, and it was dated between 9 B.C. and A.D. 78. The disturbing thing is that the Vatican had labeled this sample not as the Shroud but as a control taken from an Egyptian mummy. Presumably even the conspirators wanted to know the real truth about the authenticity of the famous and revered Shroud of Turin.

Why, then, should they fake the results? Because the Shroud could have only produced its image by virtue of enshrouding a living human being. This human being, say Kersten and Gruber, was indeed Jesus Christ. His last drink on the cross was some kind of opiate or sedative which relieved him from his pain and caused him to slump down, appearing to be dead. After the soldier had nicked him in the side with his lance, and "blood and water" had poured out of his living body, Joseph of Arimathea and Nicodemus hurriedly brought him down from the cross and took him away to a safe place. There, they anointed his wounded body with healing herbs, aloe and myrrh, and let him rest as if dead under the safety of the cloth lest any suspicious Romans might discover he had survived. Too much of Roman Catholic doctrine rests on the death and resurrection, the authors argue, to admit this new evidence into the light of day.

Earth-shaking miracles may not be so much in evidence today as they used to, either in the days of Jesus or in the days of potential medieval forgers of relics. But the ongoing dance between science and religion, of proof and counter-proof, continues— with a uniquely twentieth-century twist.

In Search of False Prophets

In the early centuries of Christianity, the miraculous was still very much in evidence, and considered to be quite in keeping with such events as the appearance of the Holy Spirit at Pentecost, the experiences of Paul on the road to Damascus, or the miracle-working capabilities of the Apostles after Jesus' crucifixion. But from the letters of John the Evangelist, we can see that there was already some suspicion that not all "supernatural" phenomena were necessarily in service of the Lord. "Many false prophets are gone out into the world," he warned. And as far as he was concerned, there was only one way to find out who was on God's side and who was not: "Every spirit that confesseth not that Jesus Christ is come in the flesh, is not of God; and this is that spirit of anti-Christ."

Right: *This painting shows the burning of books. Those books that were inspired by the devil burned, while those that had been divinely inspired escaped the flames. It was painted in the fifteenth century.*

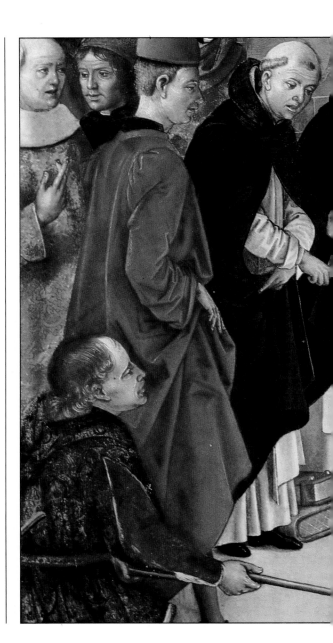

If one accepted this question as a valid test, then the issue became who was qualified to decide whether the "spirit" answering it was being honest or not. The devil, as everyone knows, is even capable of pretending to be divine. But other influential men in the early days of the Church did not see things in such black-and-white terms. Saint Augustine, for example, allowed that many extraordinary phenomena such as clairvoyance, precognitive dreams, and even materializations of phantoms and so on, could happen for reasons not necessarily either demonic or divine. But over time, the miraculous phenomena that took place outside the Church's domain—along with most forms of "spirit possession" like speaking in tongues and prophetic vision—came to be viewed with suspicion. They had the potential either to be directly competitive with the Church in gaining the loyalty and support of the people, or, within the ranks of the Church itself, to be an unruly and potentially heretical influence.

But people who had so recently been pagans could not give up the wondrous and magical aspects of religion so easily, and were soon transferring many elements of the old religion to the new. The earliest saints of Christianity tended to be those who gave up their lives for their faith, refusing to bow to pagan demands to venerate the emperor or make sacrifices to the traditional gods. Their miracles, therefore, had to do mostly with the manner of their deaths. The primary "miracle" was in many cases simply the calmness and willingness with which they met their fate. Others, more dramatically, were reportedly beaten to no effect, engulfed by flames yet not burned, run through by lances without injury, and could be despatched only by beheading.

Meanwhile, Christian hermits and monks were undergoing initiatory journeys of temptation, developing powers of divination, and attracting groups of followers sometimes against their own preference for solitude and anonymity. By the Middle Ages, the popular enthusiasm for the miraculous was on the verge of getting out of hand. The Crusades played a part in it, as fighting men returned from the Holy Land. Newly forgiven for all their previous sins because of their participation in the holy wars, they often brought back various relics of saints and martyrs that could fetch a good price as talismans against diseases and evil spirits. The less materially-minded often made presents of these relics to the local church, bringing not only further promise of salvation to the donor but adding considerably to the church's ability to attract parishioners in need of healing or comfort. The popularity of holy relics was such that at one point there were as many as six different skulls of John the Baptist being venerated at different churches scattered around Europe.

In the eyes of the church authorities, this intensity of popular fascination with the miraculous cried out for some kind of order and control—not just because of the embarrassing richness of relics, but because local

Above: *This painting shows the martyrdom of Savonarola who was burnt at the stake.*

Left: *These paintings tell the story of the martyrs St. Cosimo and St. Damiano, who were first crucified in an attempt to kill them; but when this measure failed, they were beheaded.*

saints were beginning to sprout up everywhere. Each new saintly figure brought about a new opportunity to create relics from bits of stuff that had in some way been in contact with their living bodies or their remains. If somebody didn't do something, there would soon be a special saint for every village, or even every family, and every household would be filled with sacred talismans against all kinds of diseases and bad luck. Christianity was beginning to look suspiciously like the paganism that had preceded it.

Furthermore, all kinds of heretics were on the loose, wandering around and healing people, criticizing the growing collaboration between the Church and various European monarchs, and sometimes even substituting the approved sacred rituals with new ceremonies of their own invention. In the locales where local clergy were perceived to be more interested in political power than in ministering to their congregations, these heretics attracted large popular followings. And where no organized opposition to the Church was active, the sick and troubled continued to seek out wise women, healers and diviners as they had in ancient times.

Christian priests might claim to be the messengers between the people and the divine, but miraculous events continued to happen that did not fit within the framework defined by the Church of Rome. The more spectacular of these phenomena were usually declared "diabolical" by the orthodox churchmen of

the day, and heretical wonder-workers were pursued by the Inquisition throughout the latter part of the Middle Ages. But new heresies kept popping up from time to time, continuing to cause trouble. The Camisards, for example—in the words of Pope Clement XI an "execrable race of ancient Albigenses"—were a group of Protestant Huguenots who were somehow troublesome to King Louis XIV of France in the late 1600s. When he enlisted the aid of the Church to rid his land of this "execrable race"—presumably in a fashion similar to the medieval riddance of their Albigensian predecessors—the job proved to be very difficult indeed. The Abbé du Chayla, in his report to Rome on the progress of the campaign, regretted that these people seemed to be almost invincible. Shooting them didn't work—the lead of the bullets would simply be flattened before they penetrated the skin. Torture was no good either, because if their hands were closed over burning coals they suffered no pain. He even tried to wrap a couple of them up in oil-soaked rags and set them on fire, but although the wrappings burned satisfactorily, the contents stubbornly did not.

One of the sins of the Camisards was, apparently, their failure to exhibit the pious humility required of the truly religious. One of their leaders was such a show-off that he even ordered a big pyre to be built, and climbed up on top of it to give a sermon as it went up in flames. When the fire had consumed the whole pyre, he was still standing in the middle of it,

Above: *This painting by Angelico Beato shows the torture of two victims of the Inquisition.*

Above: *A detail from Bosch's* Temptation of St. Antonio.

ranting away. A French army officer, who was quite shaken as he witnessed the whole affair, appealed to Louis to reconsider his campaign of persecution against these remarkable people and was exiled to England as a reward for his concern.

More than a century later, the invulnerability demonstrated by the Camisards arose in another group of heretics, and this time it appeared to be "contagious." During the reign of Louis XV (one wonders why the French were so specially blessed by these outbreaks) it was a group known as the Jansenists who were found to be behaving in miraculous ways. Like the Albigenses and Camisards before them, the Jansenists were renowned as healers, were unpopular with the authorities, and were gaining a large following among the impoverished masses. When a beloved deacon, François de Paris, died in 1727, his followers flocked to the site of his burial in the Paris cemetery of Saint-Médard, where they were apparently cured of cancers, paralysis, blindness and a host of other afflictions.

They also started behaving rather strangely, going into weird contortions, convulsions, spasms and so on. Worse than that, these contortions seemed to spread from one person to the next, to the point that the streets surrounding the cemetery were literally packed with the writhing bodies of men, women and children. They soon came to be called the "convulsionnaires," and demonstrated an inexplicable invulnerability to all kinds of beatings, attempted stranglings, hammerings with stones and sledgehammers, and so on. Some of them were also able to read while blindfolded, levitate, and "discern hidden things." The phenomenon continued for almost two decades, in fact, and made its way into the writings of Voltaire and the Scottish philosopher David Hume. The tortures, by the way, were conducted at least partly in response to the convulsionnaires' own request—they said that the blows they received relieved the pain of their involuntary writhings and spasms.

In the face of spectacles like these, and partly no doubt in response to the debates that characterized the Reformation and eventually led to the Protestant-Catholic split in Christendom, it was clearly past time to set up a procedure within the Catholic Church for "official" recognition of saintliness, and to declare who could properly be venerated and where. It was important to certify individual cases by studying evidence, interviewing people, and generally looking into the miracles attributed to a given candidate for sainthood. First of all, the person had to be dead—it was entirely unacceptable that anybody should be worshipped while they were still alive. After that, the person's life must be examined for sufficient evidence of piousness, and to determine whether they (or their remains, or their "spirit" in answering prayers) had been responsible for true miracles, that is miracles which supported the accepted Catholic doctrine and served some "uplifting purpose." Prospero Lambertini, who eventually became Pope Benedict XIV, was the man largely responsible for rationalizing the process of certifying miracles within the Catholic Church in the eighteenth century. And as a result of his scrupulous attention to detail one can be fairly certain today that, when an event is finally declared a miracle by the Church, it has been subjected to rigorous scrutiny, both doctrinal and scientific. As a result, there has been a noticeable decline in reports of the more astonishing miracles such as reviving the dead and walking on water, commonly attributed to saints in earlier times.

Right: The funeral of St. Orsola is depicted here in a painting by Vittore Carpaccio. She was declared a saint through the procedure of canonization that was determined by Pope Benedict XIV.

A Catalog
of Saintly Wonders

When considering a candidate's miraculous attributes for sainthood, the Catholic Church came to recognize several categories of physical manifestation of mystical states. Most of these mystical "symptoms" are also known, although without their specifically Christian content, among the Eastern religions and among shamanic cultures. But specifically Christian phenomena abound in stories of the miraculous lives of saints, including many associated with the rite of Communion. Wafers have been reported to fly off platters unaided and sail into the waiting mouths of the pious, and a chalice was once reported to have sailed across the church to touch the lips of St. Veronica Giuliani of the Five Wounds before returning to its place on the altar. St. Veronica, as her name suggests is just one of many stigmatics to be found in the Church since the first, St. Francis of Assisi, received wounds to his own body which matched those portrayed by artists on the crucified Jesus.

The mysterious appearance of these wounds of the crucifixion on the bodies of pious Catholic men and women has been perhaps one of the most controversial and thoroughly investigated phenomena attributed to divine intervention. Critics have pointed out many psychological factors common to stigmatics, including a number of attributes common to hysterical personality disorders, and the stigmata usually develop only after the sufferer has undergone several purgative illnesses that appear to be disorders of the central nervous system. R. J. M. Rickard of the *Fortean Times* has argued that the stigmata are "psychosomatically inflicted as punishment when the sufferer cannot reconcile his own sexual urges, or physical inability to adapt to the ascetic life, with his perceived ideals of Christian living."

Others have noted that the precise location of stigmata varies from person to person, often corresponding on the image of the crucified Christ with which they are most familiar. These critics suggest that if the signs were truly "divine" they would always appear in the same place. And the discovery that Jesus would have been nailed to the

Above: *In 1951 Antonio Ruffini saw an apparition of the Virgin Mary. He consequently developed stigmata through his hands and his feet.*

The miracle of Saint Jaranius

An inexplicable miracle is the liquefaction of the blood of St Janarius. St Janarius was a bishop of Benevento, beheaded by the Romans in A.D. 305. His relics included two phials said to contain his blood, and these are today held, along with his skull, at the cathedral in Naples, Italy. The phials are fastened into a silver and glass case, which cannot be opened without destroying the relics. Several times a year, the reliquary is displayed in ceremonies held in the saint's honor, and the blood, normally dried, liquefies, sometimes bubbling and foaming. On the few occasions when the blood fails to liquefy, the citizens of Naples expect a disaster of some kind, like the severe earthquake which struck Italy in 1976 just after the non-liquefaction. In 1970, Dr Giorgio Giorgi, a Naples doctor, watched the demonstration from only a yard away. He later described how the archbishop had held up the reliquary and rotated it slowly, asking the saint to produce the miracle.

"After about four minutes ... I was disconcerted to see just in front of my nose, at a distance of little over three feet, that the clot of blood had suddenly changed from the solid state into that of a liquid. The transformation from solid into liquid happened suddenly and unexpectedly. The liquid itself had become much brighter, more shining; so many gaseous bubbles appeared inside the liquid that it seemed to be in a state of ebullition."

On kissing the case, Dr Giorgi found that it was cool, proving that heating had not caused the liquefaction, which, it seems, happens regardless of the temperature in the cathedral. Sometimes the blood is already liquid when taken from the vault, at others the process of liquefaction takes more than twenty-four hours.

cross through the bones of his wrists and not through the palms of his hands, where most stigmatics show their wounds, has added further fuel to this line of argument.

Whatever the cause, though, the behavior of the wounds themselves do tend to be "supernatural." In authentic cases—that is, in those where they are not created by self-mutilation—the stigmata cannot be healed by medical science, but at the same time do not become inflamed. Many stigmatics bleed from their wounds only on significant days like Friday and Sunday, and the marks disappear completely from their bodies from, say, Tuesday to Friday afternoon. Apparently, a similar phenomenon has been observed in some devout Muslims who contemplate the wounds received by Mohammed in battle, and develop corresponding stigmata on their own bodies. But apart from this relatively rare occurrence, stigmatics are a uniquely Christian species. And while it is true that hypnotists have been able to induce stigmata in their subjects, these wounds have been at the most a bleeding through the skin, not the open wounds of religious stigmatics.

Above: *This reliquary of the holy blood at Bruges is said to liquefy every Friday at the time of the passion and death of Christ.*

St. Francis of Assisi is commonly thought to be the first stigmatic, although St. Paul did say in the closing words of his letter to the Galatians that "I bear in my body the marks of the Lord Jesus." Francis (1181-1226) was the son of a wealthy merchant, described as a "rambunctious and frivolous youth" until he was apparently literally made ill by the horrors of the civil war ravaging Italy in his youth. While praying in a church in San Damaniano in 1207 he received a vision and decided to become a wandering friar, going on to become one of Christendom's most beloved saints.

Francis of Assisi received his stigmata while witnessing a vision of Christ as he was praying outside a cave during a forty-day retreat in the Apennines. The wounds simultaneously appeared on both his hands and feet and on his side. Thereafter his wounds never healed or became inflamed, and on the hands and feet they eventually even developed nail-like protuberances of hardened, black flesh.

The thirteenth-century Cistercian nun Elizabeth of Herkenrode was another famous stigmatic, who

would bleed while entranced and seeming to witness a reenactment of the Passion and crucifixion. She also seems to be the first recorded case who developed signs of the crown of thorns on her forehead. It was about this time the first "periodic" cases of the stigmata began to take place, with these stigmatics usually bleeding copiously on Fridays only.

Saint Veronica Giuliani (1660-1727), mentioned above in reference to the flying chalice, was mistress of novices and later abbess at a convent in Citta di Castello in Umbria, Italy. First impressed with the stigmata when she was about thirty-seven years old, the wounds on her hands and feet gradually disappeared, but the one in her side remained. This particular wound was unusual in that it would open and close in response to the commands of her confessor and religious superiors. Veronica's diaries are not clear on the precise details of how they managed to discover this fact. Veronica also had an indentation in her right shoulder at the location corresponding to where Christ was commonly thought to have carried his cross. The indentation was so deep, in fact, that doctors who examined her

after her death wondered how she was able to use her right arm at all. Towards the end of her life, Veronica began to believe that her heart had been branded with emblems of the crucifixion, including a crown of thorns, three nails, and a cross. She drew diagrams showing where she felt these marks must appear on her heart, and according to reports of the physicians who performed an autopsy on her, her diagrams were accurate.

St. Teresa of Avila is another who received a wound to the heart, which is now displayed as a relic in the Spanish city of Alba de Tormes. According to Teresa's *Confessions* she received this wound from an angel she saw in a vision, who plunged a sword into her heart.

A more recent case is that of Padre Pio, currently beatified by the Church with a group supporting his canonization as a saint. Born in Italy in 1887 as Francesco, he was devoutly religious as a child, and entered a monastery in a neighboring town when he was only fifteen. There he took the name of Brother Pio, and practiced such austerities as long fasts. As a result his health broke down completely and he had

Left: *St Francis of Assisi received stigmata while witnessing a vision of Christ during a forty day retreat, as depicted in* Cima da Conegliano, *by Giovanni Battista.*

Visitations from the Virgin Mary

In 1846, two uneducated children at La Salette, near Grenoble in France, had a prolonged vision—shared in almost every detail—on an isolated hillside. The children conversed at some length with the vision, and retold with great accuracy many times the message that they said they had been given. Part of it was admonition, part consolation and affection, but the key portion for us was prophecy. The children quoted the figure as referring to forthcoming famine and sickness; 'There will come a great famine, Before the famine comes, the children under seven years of age will be seized with trembling, and will die in the hands of those that hold them; and others will do penance by the famine. The walnuts will become bad, the grapes will rot. If they are converted, the stones and the rocks will change into loads of wheat, and the potatoes will be self-sown on the lands.' By the end of 1846 potatoes could not be bought in the area. The disease phylloxera struck the grape crop. A form of cholera affecting only young children, and causing two hours of shaking and sickness before almost certain death, reached epidemic proportions. And the walnut crop failed. A vision of catastrophe certainly, but one either received from a greater power than that of the children alone, or implying that they possessed a remarkable talent for prophecy themselves.

to go home to be nursed by his mother. He eventually returned to the monastery in 1910, where he was finally ordained as a priest. Most of his life was spent in the monastery at San Giovanni Rotondo in Foggia. Pio developed his stigmata during an ecstasy he experienced in 1918 after saying Mass, where the figure of Christ appeared before him. "I was terrified when I saw him," he later said. "What I felt at that time I cannot explain. I felt as if I were going to die, and would have died if my Lord had not intervened and sustained my heart, which was pounding its way right out of my chest. The vision of the person faded away, and I noticed that my hands and feet and chest had been pierced and were bleeding profusely."

Padre Pio's chest wound was quite severe, and regularly bled from Thursday evening until Saturday, for years to come. Dr. Luigi Romanelli, chief of staff of the City Hospital of Barletta, Italy, was requested by monastery officials to study the wounds. His report states that it was his impression the wounds went right through the hands and feet, although were usually covered by a thin membrane

Above: *Padre Pio, whose stigmata bore sections of hard, blackened flesh shaped like nails.*

and were so sensitive to pressure that the doctor was reluctant to explore them too ruthlessly. Padre Pio's stigmata, like those of St. Francis, also featured the hard, blackened flesh, shaped like nails. He was much revered by those who knew him during his lifetime, and was reputed to heal people, read their minds, and on some occasions to levitate. He died on September 23, 1968, fifty years and three days after receiving his stigmata.

Besides the stigmata, there are many other miraculous and extraordinary characteristics associated with pious visionaries and contemplatives. Montague Summers lists several in his book *The Physical Phenomena of Mysticism,* including the following:

Bilocation—the appearance of the same person in two separate places at the same time. One of the more famous "bilocators" was Mary of Agreda, a seventeenth-century nun. Mary was firmly dissuaded by her superiors from talking about her visits across the sea to Indian tribes living in New Mexico, because she had never been known to leave her convent in Spain. However, on the other side of the Atlantic Father Alonzo de Benavides was writing to the Pope with a remarkable story that some local Indians had told him, of a "lady in blue" who had given them crosses, rosaries, and a chalice which they were to use in celebrating Mass. According to the report of Mary's life, the chalice was examined in New Mexico and was declared to have come from her convent. In truly miraculous bilocation, according to Church doctrine, the body is physically duplicated through the grace of God, and thus not to be confused with apparitions or "astral travel."

The luminous irradiance—the halo or "aura" often depicted in art surrounding the heads or bodies of holy persons. According to Pope Benedict XIV, this aura must appear for "some sensible duration of time" and be visible in full daylight to several persons in order to qualify as miraculous. Furthermore, it must belong to a person already known to be very holy, and be observed when they are engaged in meditation, preaching, or some other pious act.

Supernatural inedia—the ability to go for an unnatural length of time without food. It is important, needless to say, to distinguish this condition from anorexia nervosa, and to monitor the one blessed with the ability for a sufficient amount of time to make sure they are not cheating. The famous German stigmatic Terese Neumann was believed to live without taking food or water, and

soon after her inedia began she was attended full time, for a period of weeks, by two nuns who even measured the water Terese used in brushing her teeth to make sure she hadn't swallowed any.

Telekinesis—This is distinguished from clairvoyance or telepathy, both of which have been perceived by the Church as prone to being diabolical in origin. In its divine form, telekinesis is represented by Montague Summers in his telling of an event from the life of Pope Pius V when, on October 7, 1571, he abruptly rose from a meeting and went to the window and opened it. "For a moment his eyes were fixed on the heavens," says Summers, "and then returning to the table, he said, 'It is not now a time to talk any more about affairs, however pressing; it is the time to give thanks to Almighty God for the signal victory which he has vouchsafed to the Christians.'" He had apparently been granted a vision of the victory of the Christian forces in a skirmish taking place against heretics in the distant village of Lepanto. Memories of the Battle of Lepanto and the Victory of Don John may have faded from the popular mind today, but it was, at the time, of some importance to the Pope.

Demoniacal molestations—St. Christina of Stommeln was reportedly punished for her sanctity by a jealous demon who regularly battered, harassed, and beat her. Once when a pair of Dominican friars came to visit Christina she was hurled against the wall, where her head was banged against it again and again by

Above *The seventeenth-century Spanish nun, Sister Mary of Agreda, was believed to be able to be in two places at the same time, a phenomenon known as bilocation. She is seen here writing her* Life of the Virgin Mary.

an invisible force. At other times she was cut and stabbed, or besplattered with excrement. Another sufferer of diabolical abuse, St. Gemma Galgani, described a blow she received on her left shoulder that knocked her to the ground, saying years later that, "Even today I feel sick and ill from the pain."

Above: *Psychic abilities are subjected to rigorous testing. Here, the results of the screened touch matching method are carefully recorded.*

The Supernatural
Goes Underground

The various Inquisitions of the late Middle Ages were followed by the "witch hunts" of the sixteenth and seventeenth centuries, and thereafter the most sensible of secular miracle-workers kept their wondrous abilities under wraps.

Certain folk sciences like dowsing were openly employed, and reasonably harmless psychic faculties like "second sight" were tolerated, but only the most foolhardy souls would allow themselves to be publicly recognized for healing abilities or other, more controversial powers where diabolical influence might be suspected. Most scientists went to church, believed in God, and minded their own business—and even if the reality they observed was perhaps not exactly as it was set out in the Bible, they showed little of the inclination shared by their alchemist predecessors to meddle in miraculous realms. But by the middle of the eighteenth century many scientists were beginning to actively work against the miraculous underpinnings of the religious authority that had held them in thrall for so long. In

the process they began to define their own dogma to counter the "superstitions" of the Church. In place of an all-powerful God, they put the all-powerful "laws of nature," which they now had the self-confidence to presume that they understood. Nature works in certain defined and observable ways, they said, and disobedience to her laws is impossible.

The problem was, of course, that the laws of nature had a way of demanding to be redefined with unsettling regularity. Into this unsettled world entered Franz Mesmer, who, however unwittingly, brought the mysteries of the miraculous face to face with the certainties of science. In his medical school days in Vienna, Mesmer had proposed the existence of "a subtle fluid, which pervades the universe and associates all things together in mutual intercourse and harmony." In his experiments with patients he discovered, like other healers of his day, that the placement of magnets near the body of a patient seemed to have some influence over physiological functions such as the circulation of blood. The startling thing was that he also discovered that the magnet wasn't strictly necessary—he could produce the same and even more dramatic effects by simply making passes over his patients with his hands.

Mesmer, however, considered himself to be not a miracle-worker but a scientist, so he naturally tried to find scientific explanations for the results he was observing in his practice. He came up with the idea of "animal magnetism"—a force that was to be found not in minerals such as iron, but in human beings. It was entirely consistent, in his view, with his medical school thesis—in tapping into the "subtle fluid" pervading the universe, one could use it to set right any disharmonies that might exist in the human body. His views were not popular in Vienna, and Mesmer was forced to move to Paris. But there he soon found a substantial following, including Marie Antoinette. She set up a Royal Commission of Inquiry, with the then U.S. Ambassador to France, Benjamin Franklin at its head, and including many reputable and well-known scientists of the day.

The events which the investigators witnessed were startling indeed. Patients would fall into trance, or go into convulsions when Mesmer or other practitioners of his technique pointed at them with a "magnetized" rod, or a finger. They could be anesthetized in this mysterious way, and submit to normally painful invasive procedures without feeling pain. Some of them could even read while blindfolded, or play cards with their eyes taped shut. The majority of investigators, however, decided that there was no evidence of

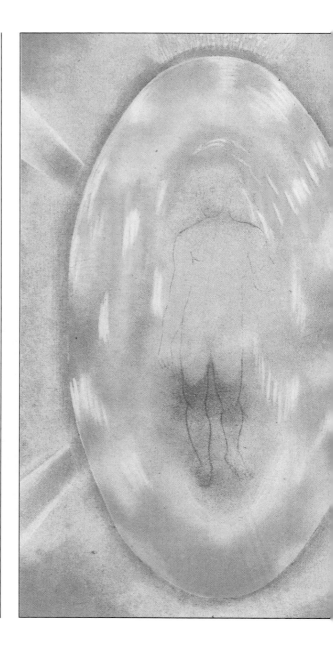

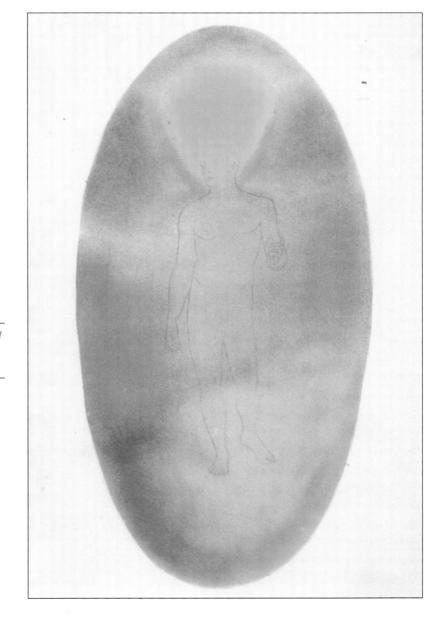

These paintings show the astral and causal bodies of two spiritually developed people.

such a "thing" as "animal magnetism" although they did admit that some powerful imaginative faculty on the part of the patients seemed to be provoked. The dissenter to this judgment was the botanist Laurent de Jussieu, who pointed out that many of the patients' reactions had taken place even when they couldn't see that they were being "magnetized." He felt the number of these instances were sufficient "to compel the admission of the possibility of the existence of a fluid or force which is exercised by man on man, and which sometimes produces a perceptible effect."

Jussieu's view, however, was not upheld by his colleagues, and the result was that the Academy of Medicine in Paris ruled that "no physician shall declare himself a partisan of animal magnetism, either in his practice or by his writings." Meanwhile an influential Lyon physician, Chastenêt de Puységur, had been conducting his own experiments and had found that one of his patients even responded to unspoken commands. This same patient, described by Puységur as "the dullest-witted peasant of the district" became, when entranced, "profound, sensible and clairvoyant." He could even diagnose other patient's disorders, so successfully in fact that Puységur had begun to use him in this capacity. Word spread of these extraordinary happenings, and other doctors in Lyon began to experiment with the technique, with equally startling results. One woman, for example, was able to read what was on a card placed on her stomach, and describe the contents of letters in sealed envelopes.

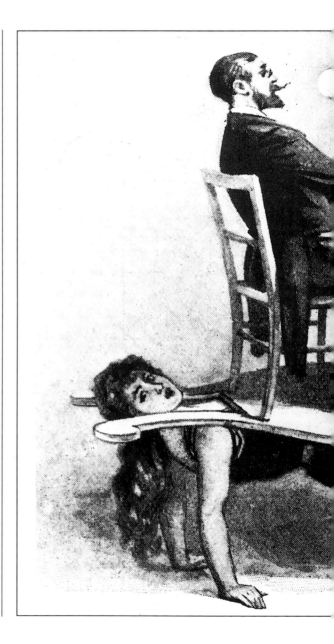

All these psychic phenomena were veering off the track envisioned by Mesmer, whose original concern had been to tap the power of his "universal fluid" simply to heal people of their ailments. Mesmer himself retired to Switzerland, and the other enthusiasts of animal magnetism were dispersed by the French revolution. But the foundations of the work survived, and were resurrected in a surge of interest in what had now come to be called "mesmerism" all over Europe and in Russia at the beginning of the nineteenth century. One Russian researcher, Professor D. Veliansky of the Imperial Academy of St. Petersburg, challenged a growing view that it was both possible and desirable to separate the "healing" and "psychic" uses of mesmerism. His research led him to the theory that there were six stages of the induced trance state, each reaching a greater depth, until, at the fourth stage the patient was entirely under the control of the magnetizer and at the fifth, the patient was able to "see" into his or her own body and recommend appropriate treatment. Obviously, the healing and psychic aspects of the technique were one and the same at this stage, so they could not be separated. The sixth, Veliansky went on to say, gave the patient access to the same territory explored by the

Left: *During the nineteenth century, séances and other paranormal occurrences captured the public imaginaion. Unusual and seemingly impossible acts found their way into the vaudeville halls and provided entertainment for the public. Here, a strong lady is depicted performing an impossible feat.*

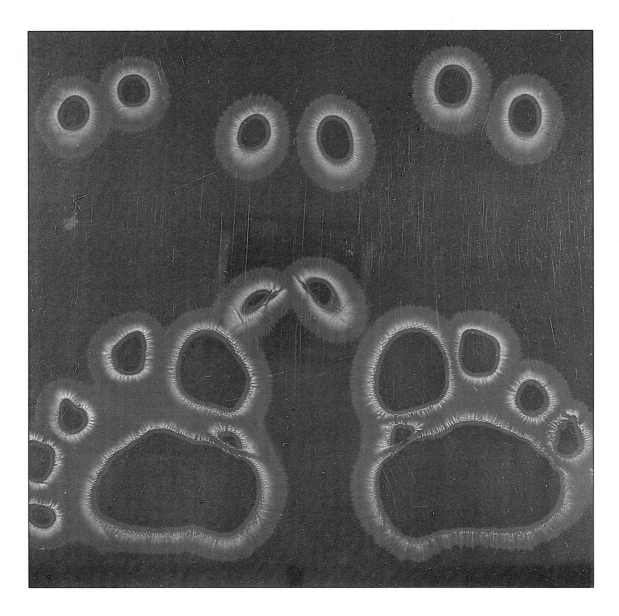

mystics, in which they were freed from the ordinary limitations of time and space and could, among other things, "see" what was happening at a distance.

Orthodox practitioners of medicine were not pleased by reports like these. And for the most part, patients did not even learn of their existence unless a fruitless search for a cure happened to drive them to the fringes of the medical community where mesmerism was being practiced. Meanwhile, a Portuguese man living in Paris was breaking one of the cardinal rules that had heretofore been tacitly observed by all practitioners of the art. His name was J. C. Faria, and he was giving public demonstrations of mesmerism in Paris, putting people into trances and making them do foolish things, and charging the audience admission to watch the spectacle. Naturally, this "show business" came under suspicion, and when one man volunteered to go on stage and, in his eagerness to prove fraud, simply pretended to go into trance and then revealed his own pretense, Faria was discredited.

The contemporaries who had known him felt that Faria was in fact not an impostor, but a sincere man who, however unwisely, had decided to alleviate his poverty by using his skills to make a living. In doing so he was, incidentally, the first mesmerist to use a method that thereafter became a kind of shorthand for all parodies of the hypnotist—he put his subjects into trance by simply repeating the word, "Sleep." Interestingly, before his entry into show business, J. C. Faria had been a priest.

Opposite: *Kirlian picture of fingers and toes, taken for diagnosis by the German naturopath Peter Mandel. This type of photography permits the practitioner to see auras which are not normally visible to the naked eye and thus to diagnose and assist the patient in healing.*

Walking through the Holy Fire

Some observers have suggested that perhaps something similar to the trance state induced by hypnosis is at work in the countless examples of fire immunity, common not only to reports about the lives of Spiritualist mediums and Christian saints, but throughout many cultures in history.

A ceremony generally known as the "fire-walk" is still practiced in many Polynesian cultures, and has gained a certain popularity in the Western world in recent times. In all of these situations, one or more guides are present whose special talents are somehow essential for the successful conduct of the ritual. Often this person is entranced for the duration of the ceremony, and it is under his or her auspices that protection from the fire is granted. It should be pointed out that it is not, however, always necessary for the participants to believe in the power of the guide, nor indeed even to want to take part in the ceremony.

Dr. William Tufts Brigham, botanist and museum curator in Hawaii, tells of an incident when he accompanied three *kahunas* (shaman-priests of the native Hawaiian religion) to an active lava flow near the volcanic mountain of Kilauea. On their way, the *kahunas* had told Brigham that they could include him in their fire immunity so that he could also walk across the lava, if he cared to join them. He at first agreed, and when they reached the site the three *kahunas* took off their sandals in preparation for saying the prayers that would enable them to walk across the lava unharmed. They told Brigham that he should also remove his boots, because the protection granted by their prayers did not extend to anyone's shoes. But by this time the sight of the glowing lava had encouraged Brigham to change his mind, and he refused.

As the first *kahuna* strolled across the glowing lava, Brigham sat a short distance from the lava flow, firmly ensconced in his boots. When the second *kahuna* started across, Brigham stood up to get a

Above: *Scenes from the legend of St Margaret depicted on a carved altarpiece in northern Germany. She is shown overcoming the dragon and being impervious to being boiled in a vat of oil.*

better look. At that point he found himself suddenly shoved from behind by the third, and forced to break into a run across the lava in order to avoid falling down on his face! Much to his relief—and accompanied by peals of laughter from the three *kahunas*—Brigham survived the crossing unharmed. His boots, however, were not so lucky: one had burned off completely, the other was in smoldering tatters, and both his socks were on fire.

Fire immunity also seems to be a thing that can arise naturally, without any ceremonial trappings, as a New York physician discovered in 1927 while on a hunting trip in the Tennessee mountains. There he met a twelve-year-old boy who could handle red-hot irons with ease—an ability he said he discovered by accident when he picked up a glowing horseshoe in his uncle's blacksmith shop. Some four decades earlier, a committee of doctors had watched as an elderly blacksmith in Maryland held a glowing shovel against the soles of his feet until it cooled, and poured melted lead into his mouth, swishing it around until it solidified. "It doesn't burn," he told the assembled witnesses. "Ever since I was a little boy, I've never been afraid to handle fire."

Left: *Firewalking, a practice that many shamans have performed for centuries, has now found enthusiasts in the West. Practitioners are protected from the burning coals through fire immunity that can be induced through trance states.*

From Spirituality to Show Business

Whether it has been Moses parting the Red Sea, Jesus walking on water, or a tribal shaman conducting a healing ceremony, there has always been a certain amount of show business involved in miraculous events.

By the middle of the nineteenth century certainly most of the sacred content of the ancient healing séances of the shamans had long been forgotten, or driven into a few isolated pockets of wilderness where nomadic tribes had been able to escape the onslaught of "civilization." Rogan Taylor, in his

Right: *This photo shows a native witch doctor during a ceremonial dance.*

insightful and unique study of the transformation of tribal shamanism into show business, *The Death and Resurrection Show*, sums up the process like this:

When radically different ways of sustaining life are adopted, as with the development of agriculture, the tribal population may increase dramatically. Individuals build permanent homes of their own, cease the communal sharing which characterized nomadic life and, at length, have something to defend. Social conditions can be created whereby tribal members become divorced from each other, and the shaman they once knew so intimately may become a blurred figure, still powerful but indefinitely so. It is at precisely such a point in the disintegration of the old nomadic way of life that the shaman's art—his skill, timing, cleverness, control and dramatic instinct—can begin to separate, to peel off, from his ecstasy. The one may even become a disguise of the other. Show business looks like the orphaned child of a divorce between art and ecstasy, forever hiding its shameful origins while, at the same time, secretly attempting the reconciliation of its separated parents.

Of course most of the world abandoned its nomadic roots ages ago. But the astounding growth of science in the nineteenth century provoked a dislocation in human spiritual life arguably as profound as that which occurs when a nomadic culture becomes, of necessity or out of choice, agricultural. In the secular world of the nineteenth century a "crisis of faith" was taking place, and that crisis was provoked by science. On the one hand, Darwin's theory of evolution had challenged man's view of himself as a special, God-created creature and on the other hand, the optimism engendered by stunning advances in science and technology had made it seem possible to create paradise here on earth. The existence of the divine, and our human need to depend on a connection with it for our own well-being, was being seriously called into question.

There was a backlash against the growing hegemony of science over human consciousness, but not necessarily in the form religious traditionalists might have hoped for. In the 1850s, for example, nearly every conversation that took place in the fashionable circles of Victorian England eventually came round to the subject of "table-turning" séances. These events sometimes featured a psychic "medium" but probably just as often a group of friends decided to conduct an impromptu experiment. The standard format of the séance involved questioning what people assumed to be "spirits" of deceased relatives or friends, and receiving answers to their questions via some kind of agreed-upon code involving "rappings" or movements of the table around which they were sitting. Even Queen Victoria and Prince Albert played with this remarkable phenomenon, and Victoria was so impressed by the results that she

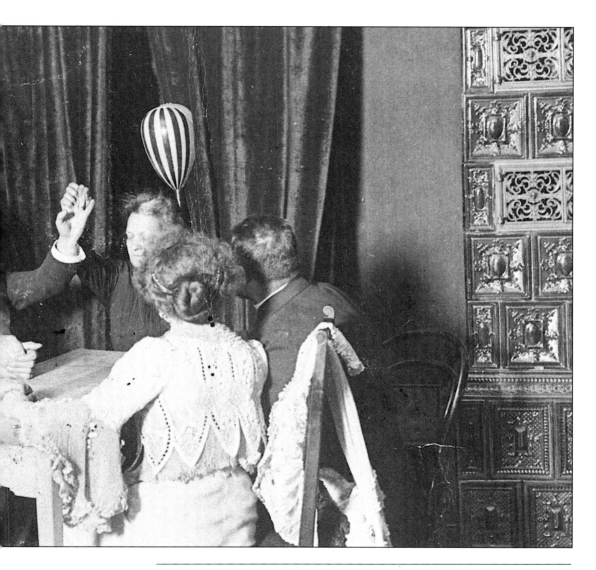

Above: *This photograph shows a séance presided over by the famous Italian medium Eusapia Paladino, in which an instrument was being levitated.*

Above: *An example of levitation. Many of these performers were found
to be frauds who used tricks to deceive the audience.*

concluded there must be some kind of "magnetism" or "electricity" that was responsible for it.

Such a novel and entertaining pastime caught on quickly, and soon the séances were happening all over Europe. In North America, the public shows performed by the Fox Sisters, two teenage girls who seemed to be able to induce what they called "spirits" to manifest similar rappings and movements of objects, had already aroused widespread interest, and even Abraham Lincoln attended a session in which he was given advice by spirits who claimed to be Benjamin Franklin and Napoleon. Horace Greeley, Elizabeth and Robert Browning, and Napoleon III and Eugenie were just a few of the luminaries of the time who sought contact with the "spirits of the departed" in this way.

The séances of the most popular mediums featured not only rapping noises and moving furniture, but also levitations, musical instruments which played by themselves, demonstrations of fire immunity, and materializations of disembodied hands that carried things around or grabbed a pen from the table and scribbled a message on a piece of paper. Some of the mediums could even provoke the appearance of entire spirit persons.

Among the scientists who dared to get involved in researching the séances, William Crookes was perhaps the most persistent and publicly outspoken. Known and respected in scientific circles for his discovery of thallium and later for his invention of the radiometer, Crookes entered his investigations in the best tradition of science, with an open mind and a determination to see whether the phenomena of the séances were elaborate deceptions, as so many of his colleagues insisted. He conducted extensive experiments with David Home, Florence Cook, and other mediums, despite the fact that he was often subjected to published attacks on his research and even his sanity by some of his colleagues. At the same time, however, his reputation for integrity and thoroughness attracted other investigators, including the naturalist A. R. Wallace, and Darwin's explorer/scientist cousin, Francis Galton. Crookes even managed to persuade Darwin himself to take an interest in the research, but a planned séance to include Darwin and Home was thwarted several times by scheduling difficulties and illness before Home finally left England never to return.

Looking back, it is often difficult to see how men like Crookes could have come to believe so passionately that all of what they were seeing was real. When we examine some of the photos from those nineteenth-century séances today, it seems obvious that many of the mediums were simply using bits of gauze and paper to produce their effects. Perhaps one factor was that photographic technology itself was

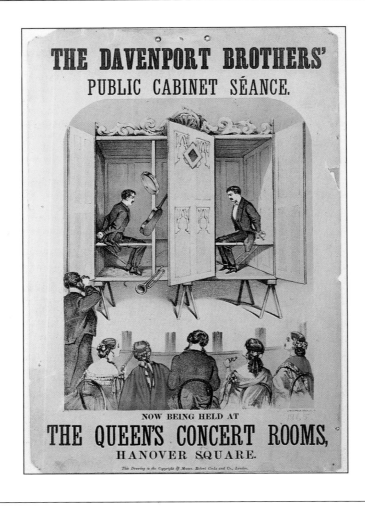

Above: Séances were particularly popular form of entertainment in Britain during the nineteenth century. Even Queen Victoria became a fervent enthusiast.

relatively new and wondrous, so people were unable to examine the evidence with the appropriate skepticism. And in every other way, precise "scientific" research was very difficult indeed.

According to the protocol of a séance, the "spirits" could refuse to come out and play in daylight, or in the presence of hostile witnesses. To touch or interfere in any way with a medium during the delicate and arduous process of materializing a spirit could have dire consequences for the medium's health. And in England particularly, it was considered impolite in the society homes where the séances were conducted to suggest that one's host or hostess was being duped by a charlatan. Many accomplished stage magicians of the time, along with the famous escape artist Harry Houdini, demonstrated that most of the phenomena at séances could be reproduced with a bit of magic and manipulation of the body's joints. But it seems that the very human desire to believe in the possibility of the miraculous often outweighed the arguments advanced by the skeptics.

Florence Cook was one of the mediums most thoroughly investigated by Crookes. Her manifestations of the spirit of "Katie King" had to originate in a dark and enclosed space, or else Katie would not "come out." The obvious explanation was that Florence herself was Katie, an effect that she could produce just by changing her costume and emerging from her cubicle. But Florence allowed herself to be searched before entering her enclosure, where she was firmly bound to a chair with ropes, which were further sealed with wax or a linen thread. After Florence had gone into trance, Katie would appear—in a gauzy white dress, while Florence was always dressed in black. After one of these manifestations, Florence was found in her cubicle but with her bindings cut, although no implement for the cutting could be found and

Florence swore that she had no idea what might have happened.

At a later séance, when sturdier bindings had been devised, a skeptical participant had grabbed at "Katie" and, finding her to be substantial, was convinced he had caught Florence in a deception. But when he rushed to the enclosure, Florence was there, somewhat disheveled but still apparently entranced and firmly bound. The skeptic's actions in the meantime had shocked and dismayed many of the other participants who saw it as a violation of the sacrosanct rules of the séance. Crookes, by this time, had been convinced of Florence's sincerity and was determined to protect her reputation. In a subsequent séance he persuaded the spirit of Katie to allow herself to be touched, and his rapturous description of her beauty and luminosity in the encounter nearly ruined his reputation forever.

David Home, meanwhile, performed most of his wonders in full view, with at least enough light in the room to rule out any deception under cover of darkness. In Home's séances an accordion played itself (with a sense of humor, apparently, usually the tune "Home Sweet Home") and it even did so during an experiment when it was sealed in a cage in such a way that he could touch it with only one hand. But Home was nevertheless hounded by allegations of fraud, and Robert Browning—some say because he was jealous of his wife's fascination with the wonder-worker—wrote a thinly veiled attack on him in his

Above: *This humorous drawing shows a scientist trying to weigh a spirit in order to determine its legitimacy.*

poem, "Mr. Sludge the Medium." But unlike most of his fellow mediums, David Home emerged from the most rigorous tests of his authenticity unscathed. Nobody ever proved that he used trickery in his work.

But in the final analysis, the séances of the mid-nineteenth century were practically all show business and no spirituality. Along with all the accounts of table turnings, levitations, spirit rappings and manifestations, came reports that the actual messages delivered by most of the "departed spirits" contacted by mediums were unbearably banal. If we

are to agree to face the chaos of the unknown that the miraculous can imply, we demand to be healed as a reward for our pains, either spiritually or physically—or at least to feel better. Not just to be entertained. And in the end, the majority of the séances of the previous century were simply not healing enough to form the basis of a new religious movement. "The only good that I can see in a demonstration of the truth of 'spiritualism'," said Thomas Huxley, "is to furnish an additional argument against suicide. Better live a crossing-sweeper than die and be made to talk twaddle by a 'medium' hired at a guinea a séance."

Scientists of the Miraculous

To explain all nature is too difficult a task for any one man or even for any one age. "Tis much better to do a little with certainty, and leave the rest for others that come after you, than to explain all things."

ISAAC NEWTON

Alongside the efforts of religious men and women to define and quantify the miraculous, there have long been efforts by those with more scientific leanings to identify the natural forces they felt must underlie extraordinary events. Albertus Magnus, Roger Bacon, Ramon Lull, and other scholarly priests and philosophers of the Middle Ages believed that the "scientific" secret of miracles might lie in the practice of alchemy. The fact that two or more substances combined could produce a new and totally different substance was no less than miraculous to these men. They devoted much time in study and speculation about any psychic or magical ingredients that might be at work in their experiments—an ingredient, most of them concluded, that must come somehow via the experimenter himself.

They were supported in this view by the translations of many texts from the Arabic, which began to flow out of the university in Toledo during the twelfth century. Among these were secret teachings from the Pythagoreans, Egyptians and Babylonians, along with the Kabbala from the mystical Jewish tradition. These medieval scientists did not, however, in any way consider themselves to be working against the Christian Church. In fact, their science was in their own minds "dedicated to the glory of God." Their search was not for a magic separate from Christianity, but to support the miraculous claims of the Church by bringing to bear whatever insights could be found in the study of the occult lore of the ancients.

The sixteenth-century scientist Cornelius Agrippa's stated aim was to "restore that ancient magic, studied by all the wise, purged and freed from the errors of impiety, and adorned with its own reasonable system" to the spiritual life of his day. His contemporary Paracelsus saw the possibility that both scientists and magicians, physicians and healers, if properly trained and disciplined, could be "holy men in God who serve the forces of nature." Agrippa and Paracelsus were nevertheless continually forced to flee from one city to the next to avoid persecution by church and government authorities. A few decades later Giordano Bruno, the

Dominican friar who insisted that miracles and magic must have a natural and scientific basis, was burned at the stake. Why? Apparently, the idea that human beings could stand on an equal footing with God was unacceptable.

Montague Summers, author of *The Physical Phenomena of Mysticism* embodies the medieval view, notwithstanding the fact that he was writing in this century. In discussing the work of Pietro Pompanazzi, an Italian scientist and philosopher whose approach to the miraculous was similar to that of Agrippa, Paracelsus and Bruno, Summers begins by reminding us that "the bigotry of science is obstinate and blind." He goes on to say that Pompanazzi "did not hesitate to spawn in his copious Works such horrible errors as the proposition that the curative power of Holy Relics consists in the faith of the pilgrim who comes to venerate them.... For Pompanazzi, a miracle is the effect of some natural cause which may in future be discovered, although as yet we do not know the material reason. Nor, I will add," asserts Summers, "are we likely to know it, until God in His own time reveals it. Which will not be here."

He goes on to tell us that Pompanazzi claimed "that man within himself is a perfect battery of marvelous force, which he can (if he knew how) energize with amazing results." And points out that "the sorcerer Cornelius Agrippa" and "the atheist Giordano Bruno" shared Pompanazzi's "subversive ideas." The argument advanced by Summers against these blasphemies is straightforward, if not entirely satisfying: God, and God alone, makes miracles. Argument finished. To suggest that ordinary humans might have within themselves the capacity to do miraculous things is tantamount to blasphemy.

In the past few decades, there has been a growing acceptance of scientific research into the inexplicable forces that sometimes enter our lives. This is due in no small part to the persistence of the researchers in conducting their experiments, responding to criticism, redesigning their experiments to satisfy the skeptics, and insisting that their findings be taken seriously. Much of the research on such phenomena as clairvoyance, psychokinesis, out-of-body travel, and so on, is in fact very "serious" indeed, and seems to be not very much fun. The laboratory conditions, statistical probabilities, and sober earnestness that characterized the experiments in the 1930s of Joseph Banks Rhine, "father of experimental parapsychology," set the tone for virtually all the experiments to follow. And although the results of these tests do indeed prove that some people are clairvoyant, able to affect material objects with their minds, or transfer their thoughts to one another without speaking, there is very little room for playfulness or spontaneity to emerge. Certainly the sacred quality that characterizes the miraculous is neither encouraged nor, one presumes, could it be "measured" in the same way one can measure how

FAMOSO · DOCTOR   PARESEL

Above: *Paracelsus, physician and alchemist, whose beliefs forced him to flee persecution wherever he went.*

many cards are correctly identified by a blindfolded subject gifted with ESP.

The scientific investigators of paranormal human abilities so far haven't been able to "explain" why some people have these gifts and others don't, or for that matter where their gifts might come from. But they have at least succeeded in creating an atmosphere where those among us who are gifted with unusual abilities are no longer subject to accusations of demon possession or witchcraft. That in itself is a tremendous contribution towards expanding our collective vision of the miraculous possibilities available to human beings. But the question remains of what we would do with these miraculous powers if we had them. If we could read the minds of others, move large objects about with nothing more than the force of our will, see through walls, or into the future, would we have the integrity and wisdom not to misuse our abilities?

At the risk of going too far afield to find a relevant example, we might look at the relatively recent experiments with powerful hallucinogens to find an answer. After 1943, when the Swiss chemist Albert Hoffman accidentally discovered the hallucinogenic properties of lysergic acid diethylamide, commonly known as LSD, among the first people to be interested in the compound were officials of the U.S. Central Intelligence Agency. Now for centuries, hallucinogens have been used by various cultures as part of sacred ceremonies because of their effect in clearing away the normal filters of the mind which enable us to function in the mundane world. The aim of clearing away these filters was to enable the participants in religious and healing ceremonies to be in direct, although chemically induced, communion with the divine, or spirit world. The first thought of those in the CIA who were interested in the possible uses of LSD was not, needless to say, to discover whether one might invite all the world's leaders to a beautiful spot and ask them to take a sacred journey together to understand God's message of love and peace. Rather, they hoped that they might be able to spray it on battlefields to confuse enemy soldiers, or administer it to taciturn captured spies to get the truth out of them. On the civilian side of things, the first generation of those who experimented with psychedelics might have embarked upon their journeys in the spirit of sacred pilgrimage, but subsequent generations have tended more and more to use the same drugs as entertainment, or even as part of demonic rituals.

The example serves as just another reminder that no matter what tools we are given — scientific technology, psychic abilities, or mind-altering drugs — the tools are not miraculous in and of themselves. Without a firm grounding in what we characterize as the "good" or the "sacred," we seem to be all too likely to misuse these wondrous gifts in one way or another.

Left: *Sir Isaac Newton, who discovered the law of gravity, was a scientist who devoted himself to identifying the natural laws under which nature functions.*

Right: *The peyote flower is a natural hallucinogen that has been used through the centuries by many tribes on the American continents, and which induces altered states.*

Part Five
Miracles for a New Millennium

C. S. Lewis, in the volume referred to at the beginning of this work, quotes a passage from The Nature of the Physical World, *by the great scientist Arthur Stanley Eddington (1882-1944): "In science," Eddington said, "we sometimes have convictions which we cherish but cannot justify; we are influenced by some innate sense of the fitness of things."*

Lewis goes on to say that this sense of "the fitness of things" also influences whether or not we are inclined to believe in a given miracle. In that sense, the "fitness" of a particular event in the overall scheme of things is the hidden, indefinable element in every definition of the miraculous. An event can be both extraordinary and impossible, and can even be declared divine, but it will not be perceived as a miracle—will not serve as a "revelation"—unless it also "fits" the needs and the consciousness of the community to whom it is presented.

In our century, it is science which has most strongly

challenged our traditional views of the "fitness" of miracles, to the point where they could be said to be an endangered species. "The modern historian," said C. S. Lewis in 1947, "will accept the most improbable 'natural' explanations rather than say that a miracle occurred. Collective hallucination, hypnotism of unconsenting spectators, widespread instantaneous conspiracy in lying by persons not otherwise known to be liars and not likely to gain by the lie—all these are known to be very improbable events: so improbable that, except for the special purpose of excluding a miracle, they are never suggested. But they are preferred to the admission of a miracle."

If we are to retain the miraculous in the modern age, then, the "bigotry of science" must be dropped. And this is indeed happening among many of the scientists themselves, although the rest of us may be, as usual, a little slow in catching up. In his book *The Nature of the Physical World,* Eddington made a remarkable statement about his subject, a statement which is still little understood today. "Recognizing that the physical world is entirely abstract and

Above: *A visionary picture by the psychic artist Heinrich Nüsslein, showing an imaginary sunken culture.*

without 'actuality' apart from its linkage to consciousness," he said, "we restore consciousness to the fundamental position, instead of representing it as an inessential complication occasionally found in the midst of inorganic nature at a late stage of evolutionary history."

In other words, he was saying that he and his scientific colleagues, in looking ever more deeply into the heart of the matter of the universe, had watched it dissolve before their very eyes. The world as we know it appears to be the way it is, only because of our ideas about it. In reality, say many scientists today, "matter" doesn't exist. And this fact is so far beyond our capacity to grasp with our minds that we have to "make it up" in a form we can cope with on an everyday level.

In biblical terms, then, Eddington and other scientists are saying that we are indeed made "in the image" of the Creator because, in fact, moment by moment we create the world in which we live. This is expressed on an individual level by such common folk wisdoms that, for example, a glass of water might be described as half full or half empty depending on the optimism or pessimism of the perceiver. And it is

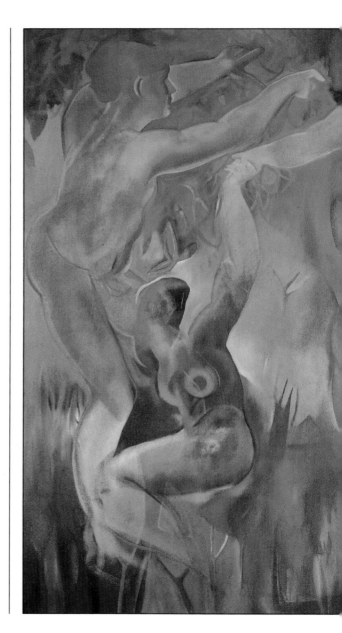

Right: The Fall *from the Michaelangelo Studies, painted by Robin Richmond shows humans about to fall from a state of grace due to their desire to acquire more knowledge of the world they live in.*

The miracle of precognition

A celebrated example of precognition occurred in Paris in the period before the French revolution. At a dinner party held in Paris just before the Revolution, attended by a distinguished company of courtiers and Academicians, the general feeling was of enthusiasm for the constitutional changes which, it was felt, could not be long delayed. Only the Marquis Cazotte remained abstracted. He had a reputation for second sight; and the others, chaffing him about his silence, pressed him for a forecast on what was going to happen. Eventually, he was induced to tell those present, one by one, what their fate was going to be when the Revolution came. Condorcet would succumb to poison, which he would take to cheat the executioner. Malesherbes, Bailly, and others would die on the scaffold; as would the Duchess of Gramont and, he feared, the highest in the land. "And I?" La Harpe– a freethinker–asked, "Do you not give me any place in this?" "Something at least as wonderful will happen to you," Cazotte replied, "You will have become by then a Christian."

The story of Cazotte's prophecy was found among La Harpe's papers when he died, a convert to Christianity, in 1803; and it was published three years later.

expressed on the level of the community, the state, the nation, and the planet, in the complex interplay and shifting balances of power and influence of individuals working together or against one another. There are times of peace and times of war, times of hope and times of despair. But whatever the times, they are shaped more powerfully by our ideas and values than by any given "force of Nature" we can name. The assertion that we "create our own reality" is not just a New Age cliché, in other words. It is a scientific truth.

Religion, on the other hand, has always addressed itself to our persistent sense that both the realm of ideas and values, and the realm of Nature, are shaped by a force transcendent to it all. But in the present century the transcendent is no longer the exclusive province of religion. Science, too, has glimpsed the possibility that there is a "ghost in the machine," that "the way things work" cannot be explained by the simple, mechanical actions that can be measured in a laboratory. "The idea of a universal Mind or Logos would be a fairly plausible inference from the present state of scientific theory," said Eddington. "In the beginning was the Word (Logos)" said John the Evangelist, "And the Word was with God, and the Word was God."

Freed from the prejudice that everything must be explainable in terms of concrete, "scientific" facts, the next challenge is to take a look at what constitutes "fitness" in defining miracles for our times. It is not the same world that Jesus entered in Palestine, where sickness was perceived to be the result of demon possession and tyrants were in the habit of ordering infants to be slaughtered. Although many of the ethical questions to which the Judeo-Christian tradition has addressed itself remain relevant today, the context in which we aspire to practice the way of life implied by that ethic is radically different.

The Judeo-Christian tradition has always addressed itself to the ethical questions, the problems of community. Love thine enemy, we are told, or "thy neighbor as thyself." But historically, our religious institutions have tended to fall short of this ideal. Instead, "enemies" have been condemned to hell at best, to slaughter and burning at the stake at worst. And miracles have tended to be viewed in a context that seeks to prove that "my God is stronger than yours." There are countless examples in the history of both science and religion of our tendency to "create a reality" based in hostility and fear rather than in harmony and love.

Miracles in our time must be appropriate to an age that has seen pictures of the earth on which we live as one shining whole, floating miraculously in a space as black and unfathomable as eternity. We must flush out and drop all remaining traces of bigotry, not just in science but in our religions as well. It is perhaps no longer appropriate to hope for miraculous events which could in any way be construed to promote one community over another, whether that be in the name of nationalism, ethnic identity, or religious affiliation.

So what is the "healing"—the "making whole" that the very word "religion" implies—required for our times? One way to get an idea is to leave the past behind, and take a look at the state of the miraculous today. This final section is devoted to that task.

Above: *This classic photograph of the whole Earth, was taken from the Apollo 17 spacecraft in December 1972. It shows Antarctica, Africa, and Arabia.*

The
"Sleeping Prophet"

It seems unlikely that Edgar Cayce during his lifetime realized that he was the herald of a new age of prophets and healers. By all accounts a modest and unassuming man, Cayce was born in 1877, the only son of a tobacco farmer living in Hopkinsville, Kentucky.

When he was sixteen, he was playing baseball when an errant pitch struck him at the base of the spine. He seemed to be all right, but later that evening Edgar began to behave in a manner completely out of character, storming around the family home, laughing uproariously, throwing things, and quarreling with people. He was sent to bed, where he quickly fell into a deep sleep. When his worried parents went in the room to check on him, the sleeping boy began to speak in a strange voice, commanding his mother to go and prepare a special poultice and apply it to the back of his head. This she did, and by the next morning Edgar was completely recovered, with no recollection of what had happened.

By the time he was in his twenties, Edgar Cayce had learned to put himself into trance—the device which earned him the name of "the sleeping prophet"—and to use the mysterious knowledge available to him in that state to help others. In doing so, he demonstrated a knowledge of anatomy and disease that was especially startling in light of the fact that he had dropped out of school in the sixth grade and the only book he read with any dedication was the Bible. He never remembered what he had said while he was "asleep" in his deep, self-induced trance. But he regularly provided detailed diagnoses of people whose medical history he knew nothing about, and often prescribed medicines that were known only to a few specialists of the day, or had been used in previous decades but were no longer available in the pharmacies. It must be said that many of the cures attributable to Cayce's intervention were of conditions rooted in the mind and psychology of the afflicted. But their physical symptoms were as often quite real and debilitating. In one of these cases, for example, a woman suffering from paralysis was told by Cayce that the roots of her problem lay in a long-

Above: *Edgar Cayce, the 'Sleeping Prophet'.*

The miracle of Close Encounters

On 1 July 1965, Monsieur M. Masse, a lavender farmer of Valensole in the Basses Alpes of France, saw a landed, egg-shaped object the size of a car, with six legs and a central pivot. Near it two 'boys' were bending over lavender plants. Masse approached stealthily through a vineyard. As he stepped from cover to apprehend the culprits, they faced him. . . . Masse saw small 'men' with large craniums, long slanting eyes, high puffy cheeks, slits for mouth and very pointed chins. A 'stick' was pointed at Masse, and he was immobilized. The creatures watched him awhile, and then 'bubbled' up a beam of light into the craft. The legs whirled, the pivot 'thumped' and the object floated away for twenty meters, then disappeared. The pivot left a muddy hole in otherwise bone-dry ground, and the legs left four marks. Close to the site all lavender plants died, and new plants would not grow.

suppressed guilt about masturbation. As soon as this cause was brought to the surface the woman made a dramatic and lasting recovery. Because of his understanding of the deep connection between mind and body, Cayce is often referred to as "the father of holistic medicine."

He was also responsible for many miraculous cures of strictly physical afflictions. His healing of the local school superintendent's five-year old daughter was one which earned him the lifelong support of the man, C. H. Dietrich. Dietrich's daughter had apparently become retarded as a result of a series of illnesses, but Cayce's trance diagnosis indicated that the real problem lay in an injury to her spine that had passed almost unnoticed at the time. A spinal adjustment was recommended, and within three months the girl was completely recovered. An even more dramatic case involved Cayce's own son, who had injured both his eyes so badly in an accident with one of his father's photographic flash lights that doctors recommended one eye be removed and considered the other to be beyond hope of repair. Both Cayce and his son were horrified at the idea, and Cayce put himself into trance to see if the "Universal Consciousness" he had come to believe supplied him with his knowledge had an alternative to offer. The prescription, involving an application of dressings soaked in tannic acid, horrified the doctors in their turn. But as Cayce saw it, it was the better of the two choices. Within ten days the boy's eyesight was fully restored.

During the forty years in which he practiced his craft, Edgar Cayce was praised by those he helped and hounded by those who were suspicious of him, especially professional medical men. He was known as "the freak" by doctors in his local community, with the notable exception of one Wesley H. Ketchum who, after his initial skepticism, began to enlist Cayce's help in diagnosing his own patients. For a long time Ketchum kept his involvement with Cayce a secret, happy with the benefits he had brought to his practice but apparently reluctant to associate himself publicly with a man his colleagues condemned as a "quack." When Ketchum finally went public by submitting a report on Cayce to a medical conference, the *New York Times* picked up the story in an article headlined "Illiterate Man Becomes a Doctor When Hypnotized—Strange Power Shown by Edgar Cayce Puzzles Physicians." The publicity was a mixed blessing: on the one hand it made more desperately sick people aware of Cayce, and as they wrote to him he began to do his famous "long-distance" diagnoses. In these, he would put himself in trance, seem to actually locate the afflicted person in space and time, and dictate his diagnosis and prescription for cure to his wife or secretary. At the institute in Virginia which carries on his work today, the archives are stuffed with grateful letters from those who were healed by this method.

The publicity also brought people to Cayce who were not so much in need of healing as curious about what other information he might have access to in his contact with the "Universal Consciousness." They wanted to know what would happen in the future, or to gain insights into the deepest mysteries of the universe, and many of Cayce's prophecies are related to such planetary concerns. He spoke of the lost continent of Atlantis, and of reincarnation—both subjects which made him profoundly uncomfortable in his waking state because they challenged his deeply-held Christian beliefs. He accurately predicted the outbreaks and endings of wars, natural catastrophes, and the political-economic upheavals of his own time, and his supporters point to predictions of the end of communism in the Soviet Union as one of just many prophecies that have been fulfilled after his death. His is perhaps the best-known prophecy that the earth is due to shift on its rotational axis before the end of this century, with catastrophic consequences for most of the coastal cities in the world.

In the tradition of all true prophets, however, Cayce was unable to use his gifts for personal, material gain. This was in any event not his inclination—he had very little concern for riches or fame. "If God has given me a special gift," he said once in declining payment for his services, "it is so that I could help others, not profit by it myself." But from time to time he was tempted in service of what he perceived to be a greater good, like constructing a hospital where more people could be treated with his methods. At other times he was exploited by those who came to see him in order to gain inside information on movements of the stock market, for example. His information on these occasions was generally accurate, but he would always suffer headaches and stomach troubles afterwards, and on some occasions would even lose his voice. If he was in any doubt about why, his source itself provided the answer: "The body should keep in close touch with the spiritual side of life," it said, "if he is to be successful mentally, physically, psychically, and financially."

Right: *This twentieth-century mystic, Osho, formerly known as Bhagwan Shree Rajneesh, attracted many Westerners who flocked to India to study meditation and seek enlightenment.*

Above: *A guru from Madhya Pradesh surrounded by his disciples.*

Journeys to the East

Edgar Cayce died in 1945, the same year that brought the end of the Second World War. His extraordinary work had taken place before the stunning post-war advances in communications technology which brought about the "global village" observed by Marshal McLuhan. Not all that many people knew about him, nor did they really know very much about what was happening in the rest of the world apart from what they heard as they gathered around their radios in the evenings. They lived in relatively homogeneous neighborhoods, and traveling great distances to see other places and cultures was a privilege reserved to the very wealthy, or the very adventurous, few.

The bombs dropped on Hiroshima and Nagasaki to end the war, meantime, seemed to have thoroughly frightened those of the species who witnessed it, and as soon as possible they shut down the fighting and set about reproducing themselves like crazy. They created a "post-war baby boom" and when these babies began to see adulthood on the horizon in the 1960s, they did their best to turn the world they were about to inherit upside down. Their search for the extraordinary was made easier by cheap transport and television, and the growing affluence and stability of their society enabled them to postpone settling down into marriage and family life on a scale that had never been possible before.

Many of the early "baby boomers" had been weaned on the writings of the beat generation—not exactly uplifting, but powerful enough in their rebellious message to set the sights of a whole generation "on the road." Once there, the more adventurous followed Hermann Hesse and made their own journeys to the East. The possibilities of bliss on earth through enlightenment, and a second chance through reincarnation if you didn't make it this time, made their way into the intellectual discourse of the West as a result. If you could "turn off your mind, relax, and float downstream," even death could lose its sting, and become just another great adventure on the road. It felt like a welcome alternative to the "life-is-a-bitch-and-then-you-die" bleakness of the existentialist philosophers and their beatnik offspring, and for many, seeking the truth in the Himalayas held more appeal than the 2-car-garage and 2.7-children formula their parents had followed in the 1950s. A new breeze of adventure was in the air.

When the children of the West alighted on the shores of the East, the East responded with a characteristic assimilative and fluid welcome. The newcomers were both naive—they didn't know that in India, for example, even the rickshaw drivers are in the habit of discussing Vedic philosophy on their lunch breaks—and impatient. Many of their Eastern hosts were more than willing to accommodate the demands of their Western visitors. Wiry sadhus with matted hair obligingly painted their visitors' pale foreheads with pigments, and graciously accepted a few rupees in return for the baptism. Maharishi Mahesh Yogi gave them mantras to chant, and hopes of bringing about world peace and levitation. Sri Aurobindo enlisted their aid in creating a paradise on earth, and hinted at the possibility of physical immortality. Satya Sai Baba rewarded their thirst for the miraculous by plucking jewelry out of the air, raining holy ash from his palms, and dissolving before their eyes only to rematerialize himself a few meters away.

Others were less willing to dispense the blessings of enlightenment so freely. Krishnamurti, elegant and austere, spent most of his life trying to tell them they were on the wrong track. "Should one seek at all?" he asked, rhetorically. "Seeking is always for something over there, on the other bank, in the distance covered by time . . . The seeking and finding are in the future—over there, just beyond the hill..

All life is in the present, not in the shadow of yesterday or in the brightness of tomorrow's hope.... So the distance between that which is to be found and that which is, is made ever wider by the search—however pleasant and comforting that search may be."

Rajneesh, on the other hand, told them that their search was only lukewarm, halfhearted. They had to be "deprogrammed" in order to create enough space for the divine to enter them, and to drop all that baggage required more commitment than just a stroll down a dusty Indian road. His meditations were strenuous, cathartic, and in his discourses he relentlessly poked fun, not only at what he saw as the superstitions and follies of Western culture, but at what he perceived to be the opportunism of some of his own countrymen. Muktananda was "just an airport luggage handler" before he became a guru, said Rajneesh, and Satya Sai Baba was "an ordinary street magician." Maharishi Mahesh Yogi had, in taking the practice of hundreds of Hindu village priests and adapting it for sale to Westerners, "raised the price of transcendental meditation from one coconut to two hundred dollars."

But whatever the shape of the particular traffic, or the price of the tolls, the alleyways between East and West opened up and became superhighways during the sixties and seventies. Kipling's rule of "never the twain shall meet" had fallen, and the planet began to look more truly "whole" as a result.

Above: *Satya Sai Baba is another Indian guru who has attracted a large following in the West.*

The Healing Touch

The meeting of East and West brought much new knowledge to its Western participants, and not the least among these were revolutionary new ways of looking at healing. For example, the principles of acupuncture, known in the Orient for centuries, began to be accepted by Western medicine along with the startling views of the workings of the body implied by those principles.

We are not, after all, just a collection of parts put together like a machine but a complex interdependency of energies and circulations of energies. And a blockage here will affect an organ there, despite the fact our logical minds tell us there should be no relationship between the two at all. Acupuncture is now in relatively common use as anesthesia, and almost every city and town in the Western world has a practitioner skilled in using it for everything from alleviating back pain to treating addictions. There has been a general "loosening up" in the view of what can be counted among the legitimate arts of making people well, despite continued opposition by more orthodox medical practitioners. In 1978, to cite a particularly noteworthy example, Italian healer Nicola Cutolo became the first "faith healer" officially allowed to work in a government hospital. And the testimony of her patients affirms the effectiveness of her "laying on of hands." It is almost as though Rupert Sheldrake's "morphogenetic field," when we look at the blueprint of Western medicine, has been radically altered by the expansion of knowledge available to us so that many new things are now being allowed to grow within it.

Barbara Brennan is one contemporary healer whose extraordinary methods typify the new approaches to healing in the latter part of this century. As a child, she used to spend hours in the woods alone, remaining as still and silent as possible in the hope that small animals and birds would approach her. Eventually, she says now, "I entered into an expanded state of consciousness in which I was able to perceive things beyond the normal ranges of human experience." She discovered she could walk through the woods with her eyes shut and "feel" the trees long before her hands actually touched them. "I realized that the trees were larger than they appeared to the visible eye"—a realization that she has now come to believe points to the fact that "everything has an energy field around it [and is] connected by these energy fields."

The miracle of the Poltergeist

An Indian poltergeist began throwing coal and stones in 1963 but later progressed to a much more varied output. The location was Karol Bagh near New Delhi, and the poltergeist was most active in December 1968, when fistfuls of dhal (pigeon peas) and gram (chick peas), lumps of coal, pedas made of moist flour, onions, tomatoes, safety matches began falling in the courtyard.' After seventeen days a reporter from *The Indian Express* came to see for himself what was happening, and wrote:

... the invisible imp keeps pelting the courtyard with his unsolicited gifts, undaunted by prayers and curses alike. Today, after raining gram and dahl on the courtyard floor in the morning, he switched over exclusively to coins later in the day. Two-paise, ten-paise and twenty-five-paise coins clinked and tinkled on to the floor from nowhere as this reporter watched in the broad daylight of five o'clock in the afternoon.

Above: *To psychic Barbara Brennan trees also had energy fields which she could sense even with her eyes closed when walking through woods.*

Left: *This sequence of photographs illustrates the various phases of a meditation technique devised by an Indian mystic.*

Brennan, after getting a master's degree in atmospheric physics and working for some time as a NASA researcher, eventually found that her extraordinary perceptive capabilities were leading her towards healing. She began to see colors and shapes around people's heads and bodies, and soon discovered that these colors and shapes could tell her something about the state of the person's health. Like Cayce, Brennan often performs her healings long-distance, and sometimes receives verbal messages of diagnosis and prescription from "what appears to be a higher intelligence than myself." By using her own "energy field" to interact with the energy fields of her patients, Brennan is able to set in motion the healing processes necessary to result in a cure.

The apparent success of healers like Brennan is hardly as yet generally accepted. But the forces of which she speaks are no longer fundamentally contradicted by the theories currently floating about in the scientific world, and in fact some theories even seem to support her and her work.

In 1947, a man named Dennis Gabor was looking down the barrel of an electron microscope when he grew as frustrated with its clumsiness and inadequacies as Newton must have been with the telescope before he improved it. Digging around in the storehouse of his scientific education, Gabor found a particular type of calculus invented by an eighteenth-century Frenchman, Jean B. J. Fourier. Fourier, in his pursuit of the particular beauty and truth offered by mathematics, had discovered a way to convert any pattern, no matter how complex, into the language of simple wave forms. Once converted, of course they could also be converted back again through a set of corresponding equations. These "Fourier transforms" as his equations are known, enabled Dennis Gabor to work out the theories that led to the development of the hologram.

Gabor's Nobel Prize for his discoveries didn't come until 1971; by then, laser technology had enabled us to produce holographic images as we know them today.

One of the extraordinary characteristics of holographic film (the kind that you shine light through to create the three-dimensional images, not the kind that holds a three-dimensional image that can be seen without any special illumination) is that if you cut it into pieces, each piece still contains the whole image. That is, the "interference patterns" created by Fourier's "wave forms" contain all the information needed to reproduce the original complex pattern, no matter which bit of them you use. The image does get less clear, the smaller the

Above: *A representation of a section of a double-stranded DNA molecule (a DNA duplex). The coils of the helix are shown as the row of white peaks, which are on average only 3.5 nanometers apart.*

pieces are in relation to the entire sheet of film. But all the basic information is there.

This news provoked sparks in a number of scientists, and "explained" some problems they had been pondering for years. To Karl Pribram, for example, it explained why people's memories worked the way they did, and even remained intact after the parts of the brain that were supposed to contain these memories had been destroyed by disease or surgery. If the brain functions like a piece of holographic film, then the memories must exist everywhere in the brain, not just in a particular place. It also explained some of the more mysterious aspects of how we learn things—not bit by bit, particle by particle, but through a complex and multi-layered interaction of "wave forms" that is much more efficient and, so to speak "holistic."

The hologram also provided a powerful metaphor for physicist David Bohm, and his theories about the nature of the universe remain controversial today. To Bohm, reality is in fact one, undivided whole. The three-dimensional reality through which we move day by day is the unfolded, or "explicate" order of a deeper level of reality he calls the "implicate" order. And this unfolding and enfolding is happening constantly—which is why he prefers the term "holomovement" to the term "hologram" to describe the universe.

The idea that "life, the universe and everything" can be seen as a hologram or holomovement is all very heady stuff, about as far removed from Newton's clockwork world—and the "common sense" notions that allow us to get up and go to work in the morning—as one can get. But the beauty of it is that it also includes these everyday realities, allows them

Right: *A hologram entitled* The Meeting, *by John Silberman. A broken wineglass is positioned in front of a holographic plate containing an image of the complete glass. When viewed from the front the images are superimposed and a complete wine glass is seen.*

Left: *This natural monument, in Western Australia, known as the Wave Rock is a remarkable example of the many 'miracles' to be found in nature.*

to exist in their own way, as illusory or "holographic" as they might be. It also, many scientists are beginning to believe, allows many other realities to exist as well—including the realities of all sorts of things that have been called "miracles." If everything, including human consciousness, has its "home" in Bohm's implicate order, for example, then why should we not be able to return to that "home"—or travel to a specific location different from the one we occupy in it—to see reality as it must be enfolded there?

If we can, some argue, then it becomes theoretically possible that a medium can "read" the past of an individual, or that a psychic healer can read the source of a disease and its cure. All they need is the gift of being able to scan the information contained in the implicate order—or, to use other languages, in Cayce's Universal Consciousness, Brennan's "higher intelligence," Sheldrake's "non-physical or trans-physical reality," or St. John's God-equals-the-Word.

Thus, in the latter part of the twentieth century, scientists appear to have just about reached the limit of taking things apart, and have started to try and put them back together again. That was the original meaning of the word "religion"—to bring together. It has always been the goal of religious mysticism, in its search for wholeness, union with the source, or with the divine. As Rene Weber points out in the introduction to her collection of interviews, *Dialogues With Scientists and Sages:* "It is mysticism, not science, which pursues the Grand Unified Theory with ruthless logic—the one that includes the questioner within its answer. Although the scientist wants to unify everything in one ultimate equation, he does not want to unify consistently, since he wants to leave himself outside that equation." She also points out that with the advent of quantum mechanics, where "the observer is the observed," this separation starts to break down. Ultimately, as Weber so eloquently states, "A parallel principle drives both science and mysticism—the assumption that unity lies at the heart of our world, and that it can be discovered and experienced by man."

Right: *Fractal geometry demonstrates order and pattern in apparently irregular, random structures, such as coastlines.*

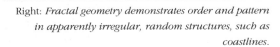

The miracle of UFO sightings

NEAR ROSEDALE, IN VICTORIA, AUSTRALIA

During the night of September 30, 1980, a farmhand was woken up at night by cattle bellowing, he went out and saw a domed UFO moving just above the paddock. It had no wings or tail, and he saw orange and blue lights on the fifteen-foot-tall craft. It hovered over a water tank before landing in the paddock.

The farmhand drove over to it on his motorcycle, and as he approached it, he heard a whistling noise and felt like jelly. As he watched from a distance of forty feet, the UFO made a screaming noise and took off, sending out a blast of hot air. The following day he found the landing site clearly marked, and 10,000 gallons of water had gone missing from the tank.

Prophets for a New Age

"In primitive man," says Mircea Eliade, "as in all human beings the desire to enter into contact with the sacred is counteracted by the fear of being obliged to renounce the simple human condition and become a more or less pliant instrument for some manifestation of the sacred." Edgar Cayce, in common with most of his biblical counterparts, exhibited just such a reluctance to accept his prophetic mission at the beginning. "Why would God pick out somebody like me," he wondered aloud, "and give him this strange power?" And when for the first time he had used his "strange power" to correctly diagnose and prescribe a cure for a friend, the osteopath and hypnotist Al Layne, Cayce avoided the man for weeks afterwards, seemingly almost embarrassed by what had transpired.

In becoming a "more or less pliant instrument" for the Universal Consciousness to express itself, Cayce showed considerably more reluctance than some of those who have succeeded him. "Channelers"

abound these days, claiming to speak on behalf of entities whose names have an ancient and sometimes even biblical ring to them: Seth, Lazaris, Ramtha, Emmanuel. Most of them do not claim to be God, but more often representatives of lost civilizations, or councils of wise discarnate spirits. Some claim to originate neither in the past, nor even on this planet, but to be extraterrestrial beings trying to intervene to save a blind and earthbound humanity from self-destruction. All in all, their messages tend to be appropriate to an age of quantum physics, holographic theories of reality, and an ecumenical view of human spirituality. We create our own reality, they say, and God lives within each and every one of us waiting to be realized.

Apart from some of the more outlandish manifestations of exotic personalities with mysterious tales of their origins, the entities hosted by most channelers deliver messages consistent with the eternal truths and wisdom traditions of Christianity and other religions, stressing the importance of love and viewing life as a learning process. Other messages are more exotic: "We are individualized portions of energy," says Seth, the entity channeled by Jane Roberts from 1963 until her death in 1984, "materialized within physical existence, to learn to form ideas from energy and make them physical." Lazaris, channeled by Jach Pursel, says on the other hand that we are here to eventually learn that we all exist simultaneously in many dimensions and could, if we only knew how, travel between them at will. Lazaris' purpose in talking to us is to help us be better able to solve our own problems, create better realities, and remind us that we can grow not just through pain and fear but through love and joy. Ramtha, channeled by J. Z. Knight and made famous by Shirley MacLaine in her book, *Dancing in the Light*, is a former inhabitant of the lost continent of Atlantis whose early messages of love and creativity have gradually given way to predictions of earthquakes and other natural calamities similar to those foreseen by Cayce.

Right: *Mediumistic artwork by Clara Schuff who died in 1988. Her art showed hieroglyphs, symbols and images from highly developed civilizations long disappeared from the Earth. She also spoke their languages.*

Epilogue
Believing the Impossible
Before Breakfast

One notable exception to the more vague, ecumenical language of most "New Age" channeled material is A COURSE IN MIRACLES, *a hefty self-study manual that uses explicitly Christian imagery and language—although with a decidedly Gnostic bias—to make its point.*

This is despite the fact that its "medium," Dr. Helen Cohn Schucman was an atheist and psychology professor at Columbia University when the massive volume of work was received as "a kind of inner dictation." Her task had been foreshadowed by years of "mental pictures" or visions that would appear to her in black and white.

In the 1960s they began to take on color and movement, and soon she was hearing a "Voice" which provoked her to fear that she might be going insane. In October 1965, her mission finally became clear. "This is a course in miracles," the Voice said. "Please take notes." Schucman obeyed, although often with considerable reluctance, for the next seven years. She even disagreed with much of the

material, but every time she was tempted to change the words being dictated to her she found she could not do it. When the work was finally finished, the Voice told Schucman to set it aside, and that somebody else would come along who would know what to do with it. Three years after *A Course in Miracles* was completed, Schucman met Judith and Robert Skutch, who established the Foundation for Inner Peace and published the *Course* in three separate volumes consisting of a Text, a Workbook for Students and a Manual for Teachers. In 1985, the Foundation also published the entire Course in a single volume edition, and also licensed Penguin Arkana to do the same in England. When the *Course* was first published, students began to form independent study groups that met for the purpose of reading the material, discussing it and putting it into practice. Currently there are over 1,500 such groups in existence. It is interesting to note that the books were distributed strictly through word-of-mouth, and that over a million copies are now in print. Schucman's identity, at her own request, was not revealed until after her death in 1981.

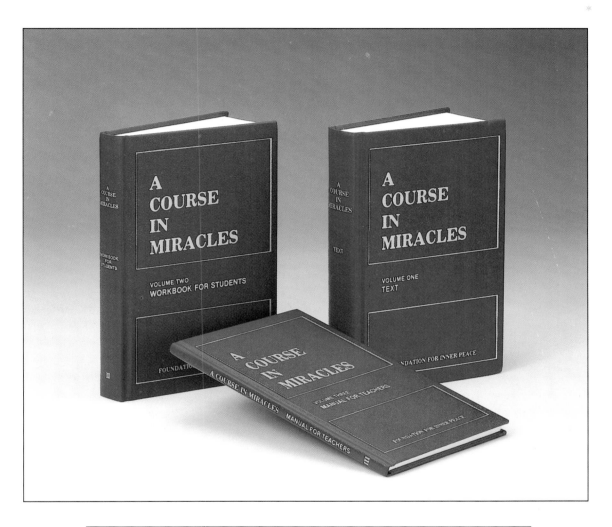

Above: *A photograph of the three-volume work,* A Course in Miracles, *which was channeled by Dr. Helen Cohn Schucman. It has provided inspiration for many thousands of people.*

Above: *A photograph of the American psychic Jeane Dixon.*

A Course in Miracles clearly embraces the notion that we create our own reality, both individually and collectively—and asserts that the problem is that we have been creating it from a perspective of fear and scarcity rather than from one of love and abundance. "Miracles enable you to heal the sick and raise the dead because you made sickness and death yourself," says the text of the *Course* in the first chapter, "and can therefore abolish both. You are a miracle, capable of creating in the likeness of your Creator. Everything else is your own nightmare, and does not exist." Jesus, as the "Son of God," came to show us what is possible to all of us if we can just "change our minds" and function with love rather than fear. We are all "Sons of God," in other words, but we have forgotten it. Jesus, along with other great sages and teachers of humankind, demonstrate in the flesh that it is possible to remember it, and they offer the rest of us the opportunity to do the same.

It is a message with tremendous appeal for a generation that has tried protest and politics, dropping out and drugs, and even a relentless pursuit of material possessions, and found them all to be lacking. Marianne Williamson, a well-known interpreter of the Course who is herself a member of the "baby boom" generation, explains its appeal to her contemporaries in her book, *A Return to Love:* "We are a Prodigal Son generation," she says. "We left home and now there's an excitement in the air because we're back. We did everything to violate love, of ourselves and others, before a life of wholesomeness began to attract us. That's not our shame but our strength. There are certain doors we don't have to go through—[not] because a false moralism said not to, but because we opened them already and we know they lead nowhere. Oddly enough, this gives us a kind of moral authority. We speak from experience. We've done the dark side. We're ready to move on. We're attracted to the light."

Elsewhere in the same book, Williamson clearly expresses what many of her generation only vaguely sense, that not only the course of the future but perhaps the very possibility of its existence lies in their hands: "The decisions we make today, individually and collectively, will determine whether the planet goes to hell or goes to Heaven. One thing, however, is sure: we are the transitional generation. The critical choices lie in our hands. Future generations will know who we were. They will think of us often. They will curse us, or they will bless us."

It is the intent of Williamson and other teachers of *A Course in Miracles* to be blessed. And their work is nothing less than to create the conditions for the grandest miracle of all, the reunion of heaven and earth in a Paradise so loving and healing that the miracles of the past will no longer be required.

Above: *The spider in her web.*

The ET Factor

A COURSE IN MIRACLES *represents one stream of "miracle thinking" today, which places the responsibility for the miraculous squarely on the shoulders of each human being. Another significant stream still hopes for intervention from above. But, reflecting the scientific biases of the twentieth century, this "above" is perceived not as some heavenly, other-dimensional realm, but the literal, physical "above" of the stars and planets in the sky.*

In earlier times, enough of our own planet still remained unknown and unexplored that writers were free to invent fantastic lands beyond the seas, where marvelous adventures were to be had. They could put all their utopian dreams for humanity, or indeed their worst nightmares about where humanity was headed, into fictional societies that existed right here on earth. Nowadays, we have pretty much discovered all the people and societies that exist here on our own planet. If writers want to invent new societies and ways of life they tend to write "science fiction," placing their characters on other planets, or in other scientifically plausible dimensions. If *A Course in Miracles* represents the religious side of the modern human personality, then the growing popularity of science fiction must represent the scientific side. And if the popularity of science fiction is any indication, vast numbers of humans have pretty much given up hope that they can solve their own problems here on earth. If we want to find Paradise, they seem to be saying, we'll have to import it from a civilization more advanced than ours. And if we want to find a civilization more advanced than ours, our only hope is to leave this planet and look for it elsewhere.

A Gift of Prophecy, the 1965 biography of the American psychic Jeanne Dixon, was author Ruth Montgomery's first bestseller, and was not to be her last. Montgomery herself had been interested in all things paranormal since the 1950s when she was attending séances in Florida, Washington, and Pennsylvania. She had already discovered in herself a talent for automatic writing, and despite the fact she was much older than most of her fans she went on to write about life after death, reincarnation, and other subjects popular to the children of the New Age.

In 1985 Ruth Montgomery made the startling assertion, at the behest of her "guides" in the spirit

Above: *ET, the title character in Steven Spielberg's movie, captured the imagination of many people. One of the biggest grossing movies of all time, it shows the readiness of audiences to believe in the possibility of alien life.*

THE OFFICIAL MOVIE MAGAZINE

STAR TREK V

THE FINAL FRONTIER

THE ULTIMATE TRIP
Kirk, Spock & McCoy
venture where no man
has gone before

Deluxe
Collectors'
Edition

Meet
Sybok, the
passionate
Vulcan

The Art of THE
FINAL FRONTIER

The spectacular
special effects

Enterprise
crew portraits

Right: *Science fiction has
attracted a huge
following. The 'Star Trek'
television series and
movies have countless fans
who have loyally followed
the crew of the starship
Enterprise on its journey of
discovery.*

world, that extraterrestrials were present on earth to train the upcoming leaders of the *real* New Age which was to follow the disruption of the earth's rotational axis predicted by Cayce and others. This book, titled *Aliens Among Us,* was a natural progression from her 1979 work, *Strangers Among Us.* In that book Montgomery had brought the notion of "walk-ins" to the realm of public discourse.

A "walk-in" is, according to Montgomery, a highly developed discarnate entity who takes over the body and personality of an incarnate adult. At any one time there might be hundreds of thousands of such beings among us, but they generally keep their identities hidden. Their purpose is to help raise the spiritual consciousness of the planet so that we might be better equipped to cope with the millennial upheaval when it takes place, and thereby make a relatively smooth transition to the new era of peace and understanding that lies beyond it. Most walk-ins reportedly come from other planets (presumably more advanced than ours) although some originate in the "sixth dimension." They are not, as one might suspect, simply the products of the current space age here on earth. Jesus Christ himself was a walk-in, along with his father Joseph and other luminaries such as Moses, the German mystic Meister Eckhart, Christopher Columbus, many of the founding fathers of the United States, Abraham Lincoln, Mahatma Gandhi, and Albert Einstein.

Montgomery is by no means alone in attributing miraculous powers and interventions to extraterrestrials. In several of his books, including *Chariots of the Gods*, Eric Von Daniken theorizes that travelers from space have visited Earth from time to time to give the evolutionary progress of its inhabitants a little nudge. Phyllis Schlemmer, who divides her time between Florida and Israel, channels messages from a "Council of Nine" who are described in the introduction to *The Only Planet of Choice: Essential Briefings from Deep Space*. The book, compiled Schlemmer's sessions with "Tom" who in turn relays messages from the Council describes this group as "a high-level circle of great beings who exist outside the Universe of space and time." They are not really extraterrestrials as we normally think of them, but live in another dimension where they "are on close terms with that Beingness-Consciousness-Happiness we frequently call 'God.'"

As the title of the book suggests, Schlemmer's Council says that Earth is one of many places available for habitation in the universe, but it is only here that the inhabitants have absolute freedom to construct reality as they see fit. Unfortunately, we have lost sight of the bigger picture and too many of us are hanging around refusing to evolve to another stage. In doing so, we are interfering with the overall energy balance and retarding the evolution of the universe. In communicating through Schlemmer, the Council of Nine is trying to help us get out of the trap we have put ourselves in. If we don't manage on our own, they say—a prediction echoed by others drawn to the possibilities of extraterrestrial interventions—they will descend from the sky in their glowing silver discs and deal with us face to face.

What to make of all this talk of planetary upheavals, healings of auras, extraterrestrial saviors and alien-trained leaders of a New Age? It's enough to send one scurrying back to the Bible, enough to make one long for the good old days when manna was falling from the sky and water was turning into wine. These old familiar miracles look absolutely *normal* compared to the prospect of strange discarnate entities dropping in on us from deep space to tidy up the planet because we've made such a mess of it on our own.

But are They Really so Different?

It is a psychological truth that the best way for a disturbed psyche to be healed is for the person to be able to encounter the repressed contents of the unconscious in a safe environment, to bring them to the light of day, and thereby be able to purge them from the psychic system, as it were. The same principle applies to the healing of many physical complaints—a wound buried under a superficial layer of healthy skin is not capable of healing until it is exposed and cleansed. And no dis-ease, whether spiritual, physical or mental, will leave us undisturbed for long. If we don't tend to it, it makes a fuss in order to get our attention.

Our culture has tried, for a rather long time, to suppress the human longing for the miraculous, and to deny the reality of a transcendent force that we have most often called God. To recall the words of C. S. Lewis again, we have for some time lived in a world where "the mass is still simple and the seers are no longer attended to" and we have indeed achieved a great deal of "superficiality, baseness, [and] ugliness." Our recognition of this fact is evident in the growing sense that, even though we might have lessened the prospect of nuclear war in the past few years we may yet be facing extinction. It is natural in times like these for the human animal to look for miraculous intervention in its affairs. That the images of the "transcendent force" behind the hoped-for miracles can take the shape of space aliens is both a rather comical reflection of our culture, and a rather tragic indication of the failure of traditional institutions to provide meaningful solutions to our sense of helplessness and despair.

But at the same time there is cause for celebration and hope. The very fact that so many people are searching, and that even the most outlandish of their discoveries by and large get a respectful, if not entirely credulous, hearing, shows that we have at least made some progress in our capacity to love our neighbors since the times when Christ was crucified. Yes, we do continue to do horrible things to each

Above: *A desert scene similar to those that provide the setting to many of Carlos Castaneda's books.*

"And what is real?" don Juan asked me very calmly.

"This, what we're looking at, is real," I said, pointing to the surroundings.

"But so was the bridge you saw last night, and so was the forest and everything else."

"But if they are real, where are they now?"

"They are right here. If you had enough power you could call them back. Right now, you cannot do that because you think it is very helpful to keep on doubting and nagging. It isn't, my friend, it isn't. There are worlds upon worlds, right here in front of us."

CARLOS CASTANEDA, *THE POWER OF DREAMING*

other as a species—no one could deny that in the face of the Holocaust and countless other genocidal activities that have taken place in recent human history. But let us remind ourselves that these actions are not generally perpetrated by people who not only seek guidance from their seers and sages but actually try to put into practice their messages of love and healing.

The "fitness" of all miracles, in the final analysis, is determined by the fact that they promote this love and healing, this unity of humanity under God — however that God is defined. "Reflection tells us that we are in sympathetic relation to each other," said the Greek philosopher Plotinus. "Suffering, overcome, at the sight of pain; naturally drawn to forming attachments—all this can be due only to some unity among us. And if spells and other forms of magic are efficient, even at a distance, to attract us into sympathetic relations, the agency can be no other than the one Soul. A quiet word induces changes in a remote object, and makes itself heard at vast distances—proof of the oneness of all things within the one Soul."

It is a common belief that all of us, in the ancient past, occupied a sacred landscape very much like the Garden of Eden. There was no need for scientists to develop a "unified theory" because the unity of all things was self-evident, transparent. Black Elk, the famous Lakota medicine man, saw in his vision "the shapes of all things in the spirit, and the shape of all shapes as they must live together as one being." The sacred pipe ceremony of his tribe always began with the words, "We are all related." The healer, the seer, the "holy person" functioned at the center of this seamless whole, able to influence it in countless ways. This ability was both extraordinary and ordinary, since all persons were assured of their connection with the divine even if their own powers did not extend to the ability to perform miracles.

We have long since lost touch with that magical childhood of humanity, and have passed through a long and troubled adolescence. If we are all to become wise, as C. S. Lewis suggests might be the aim of what he calls a daring experiment being carried out in our times by the "Power which rules our species," then on the successful completion of the experiment we can expect to enter the world of childlike wonder that belongs to the truly old and wise. It will be an even richer world than that of childhood, because we will enter it not only knowing the difference between good and evil, but having the wisdom to choose the good.

"Miracles...should be involuntary," says the text of *A Course in Miracles*. "They should not be under conscious control. Consciously selected miracles can be misguided."

"Miracles are natural," it goes on to say. "When they do not occur something has gone wrong."

Above: *Peter Pan, the eternal youth,
inspires us to retain the innocence and spontaneity
of children in viewing life.*

carried out in our times by the "Power which rules our species," then on the successful completion of the experiment we can expect to enter the world of childlike wonder that belongs to the truly old and wise. It will be an even richer world than that of childhood, because we will enter it not only knowing the difference between good and evil, but having the wisdom to choose the good.

"Miracles . . . should be involuntary," says the text of *A Course in Miracles.* "They should not be under conscious control. Consciously selected miracles can be misguided."

"Miracles are natural," it goes on to say. "When they do not occur something has gone wrong."

A Course in Miracles. Foundation for Inner Peace, Tiburon, California: 1975; Penguin Arkana, New York: 1985.

Adare, Lord. *Experiences in Spiritualism with D.D. Home*. London Society for Psychical Research, London: 1924.

Brennan, Barbara. *Hands of Light*. New York: Bantam Books, 1988.

Bohm, David. *Wholeness and the Implicate Order*. London: Routledge & Kegan Paul, 1980.

Davies, Paul, and John Gribbin. *The Matter Myth*. New York: Viking Penguin, 1991.

Dodd, C. H. *The Interpretation of the Fourth Gospel*. Cambridge & New York: Cambridge University Press, 1953.

Eliade, Mircea. *Shamanism*. Princeton, New Jersey: Princeton University Press, 1964.

Gribbin, John. *In The Beginning*. New York: Viking Penguin, 1993.

Guiley, Rosemary Ellen. *Harper's Encyclopedia of Mystical and Paranormal Experience*. San Francisco: Harper San Francisco, 1991.

Haraldsoon, Erlendur. *Modern Miracles: An Investigative Report on Psychic Phenomena Associated with Sathya Sai Baba*. New York: Fawcett Columbine Books, 1987.

Haynes, Renee. *Philosopher King: The Humanist Pope Benedict XIV*. London: Weidenfeld & Nicolson, 1971.

Hiley, Basil J. and F. David Peat, eds. *Quantum Implications*. London: Routledge & Kegan Paul, 1987.

Inglis, Brian. *Natural and Supernatural: A History of the Paranormal*. Kent, U.K.: Hodder & Stoughton, 1977; Bridport, Dorset, U.K.: Prism Press, 1992.

Kersten, Holger and Elmar R. Gruber. *The Jesus Conspiracy: The Turin Shroud and the Truth about the Resurrection*. Dorset, U.K.: Element Books, 1994.

Kreiser, B. Robert. *Miracles, Convulsions, and Ecclesiastical Politics in Early Eighteenth-Centuryd Paris*. Princeton, New Jersey: Princeton University Press, 1978.

Lewis, C. S. *Miracles: A Preliminary Study*. London: Collins, Fount Paperbacks, 1960.

Montgomery, Ruth. *Strangers Among Us*. New York: Fawcett Books, 1984. *Aliens Among Us*. New York: Fawcett Books, 1986.

Reed, Henry. *Edgar Cayce on Mysteries of the Mind*. New York: Warner Books, Inc., 1989.

Rooney, Lucy and Robert Faricy. *Mary, Queen of Peace*. Dublin: Fowler Wright Books, 1974.

Schlemmer, Phyllis V. and Palden Jenkins. *The Only Planet of Choice: Essential Briefings from Deep Space*. Bath, U.K.: Gateway Books, 1993.

Sheldrake, Rupert. *The Presence of the Past. Morphic Resonance and the Habits of Nature*. New York: HarperCollins, 1989.

Siegel, Bernie S. *Love, Medicine, and Miracles*. New York: Harper & Row, 1986.

Smith, Joseph Jr. *The Pearl of Great Price*. Salt Lake City, Utah: The Church of Jesus Christ of Latter-day Saints, 1972.

Stern, Jess. *Edgar Cayce, The Sleeping Prophet*. New York: Bantam Books, 1968. *Edgar Cayce, A Prophet in His Own Country*. New York: Bantam Books, 1968.

Summers, Montague. *The Physical Phenomena of Mysticism*. London: Rider & Company, 1950.

Swinburne, Richard, ed. *Miracles*. New York: MacMillan, 1989.

Talbot, Michael. *The Holographic Universe*. New York: HarperCollins and HarperPerennial, 1991, 1992.

Thiering, Barbara. *Jesus the Man*. New York: Doubleday, 1992.

Thurston, Herbert. *The Physical Phenomena of Mysticism*. London: Burns Oates, 1952.

Tillich, Paul. *Systematic Theology*. Chicago: University of Chicago Press, 1951.

von Daniken, Erich. *Chariots of the Gods? Unsolved Mysteries of the Past*. Translated by Michael Heron. New York: Souvenir Press, 1969.

Walsh, William T. *Our Lady of Fatima*. New York: Macmillan, 1947.

Weber, Renee. *Dialogues with Scientists and Sages*. London: Routledge & Kegan Paul, 1985.

Weinberg, Steven Lee, Ph. D., ed. *Ramtha*. Eastsound, WA.: Sovereignty, Inc., 1986.

Williamson, Marianne. *A Return to Love: Reflections on the Principles of A Course in Miracles*. New York: HarperCollins, 1992; New York: Harper Perennial, 1993.

Biblical quotations are taken from the King James Version of *The Holy Bible*.

ACKNOWLEDGMENTS

Scala, Firenze: 2, 5, 11, 15, 16, 27, 52, 58, 70, 72, 74, 114, 122, 124, 127, 129, 130, 134, 137. E.T. Archive, London: 7, 9, 19, 31, 41, 48, 73, 116, 121, 133, 148, 219. The Mansell Collection, London: 12, 81, 86, 93, 104, 173. Mary Evans Picture Library, London: 20, 44, 60, 150, 151, 183. Bridgeman Art Library, London: 23, 33, 50, 55, 83, 95, 142, 166, 171. Bodleian Library, Oxford: 25. Premgit: 28, 188. Science Photo Library, London: (Lifesmith Classic Fractals 34; Petit Format 37), 181, (Lawrence Berkeley 197; Eve Ritscher Assoc/John Silverman 199; Hank Morgan 203), 212. Gianluca De Santis: 38, 98, 175. C.M. Dixon Colour Photo Library, Kent: 42, 46, 77, 157. Church of the Latter Day Saints: 56. Michael T. Holland: 62, 193. Fortean Picture Library, Wales: 64, 68, 91, 100, 101, 109, (Torro 112; Dr Elmar R. Gruber 139, 154, 163, 177, 207), 141, 145, 147. 168. Werner Forman Archive, London: 79. Ann & Bury Peerless: 106, 158. Sonia Halliday Photographs: 110, 119. Hulton Deutsch, London: 152, 160, 164. Robin Richmond: 178. Osho International Foundation: 187, 194, 195. Impact Photos, London: 200. Foundation For Inner Peace, California: 209. Toronto Globe & Mail, Toronto: 210. BFI Stills, London: 215. Star Trek Magazine: 216. Adventure Comics: 221.

Dialogues with Scientists and Sages by Renee Weber. Reprinted by permission of Routledge & Kegan Paul, London: p.202. *A Return to Love: Reflections on the Principles of A Course in Miracles* by Marianne Williams. Reproduced by permission of HarperCollins Publishers, New York: p.211. *The Art of Dreaming* by Carlos Castaneda. Reproduced by permission of HarperCollins Publishers, New York, 1994: p.219.